CHRISTMAS WITH *Victoria*

CHRISTMAS WITH *Victoria*

Oxmoor
House.

Oxmoor House, Inc.
Book Division of Southern Progress Corporation
P.O. Box 2463, Birmingham, Alabama 35201

Library of Congress Catalog Card Number: 97-65914
ISBN: 0-8487-1641-8
ISSN: 1093-7633
Manufactured in the United States of America
First Printing 1997

We're here for you!
We at Oxmoor House are dedicated to serving you
with reliable information that expands your imagination
and enriches your life. We welcome your comments
and suggestions. Please write us at:

> Oxmoor House, Inc.
> Editor, Christmas with *Victoria*
> 2100 Lakeshore Drive
> Birmingham, AL 35209

To order additional publications, call 1-205-877-6560.

Victoria

Editor-in-Chief: Nancy Lindemeyer
Editorial Director: Deborah Beaulieu
Art Director: Susan Maher
Executive Editor: Mary Aurea Morris
Deputy Editor: Daniel D'Arezzo
Editorial Operations Manager: Marie-Lucie Charlot
Market Editor: Susan George

Oxmoor House, Inc.

Editor-in-Chief: Nancy Fitzpatrick Wyatt
Senior Homes Editor: Mary Kay Culpepper
Senior Foods Editor: Susan Carlisle Payne
Senior Editor, Editorial Services: Olivia Kindig Wells
Art Director: James Boone

Christmas with *Victoria*

Editor: Adrienne E. Short
Associate Art Director: Cynthia R. Cooper
Editorial Assistant: Allison D. Ingram
Designer: Rita A. Yerby
Copy Editors: Jacqueline B. Giovanelli, L. Amanda Owens
Writer: Virginia Gilbert Loftin
Contributing Editors: Julie Fisher, Caroline A. Grant,
    Shannon S. Jernigan, Susan Hernandez Ray, Lisa H. Talley
Senior Photographers: Jim Bathie, John O'Hagan
Photographers: Ralph Anderson, Brit Huckabay
Senior Photo Stylists: Kay E. Clarke, Katie Stoddard
Photo Stylists: Virginia R. Cravens, Linda Baltzell Wright
Director, Test Kitchens: Kathleen Royal Phillips
Assistant Director, Test Kitchens: Gayle Hays Sadler
Test Kitchen Staff: Molly Baldwin, Susan Hall Bellows,
    Julie Christopher, Natalie E. King, Elizabeth Tyler Luckett,
    Jan Jacks Moon, Iris Crawley O'Brien, Jan A. Smith
Publishing Systems Administrator: Rick Tucker
Production Director: Phillip Lee
Associate Production Manager: Vanessa C. Richardson
Production Assistant: Faye Porter Bonner

Contents

Foreword

~⚜~

We await Christmas with joy and wonder, and we hope to share that spirit with you in this book, **Christmas with *Victoria*.**

We are pleased to offer ideas for gifts, decorations, menus, and more, all designed to help you make this time unforgettable for you and those you love. This is a hands-on book, with projects that can be mastered by a novice or taken to new heights of creativity with your personal touch. Beautiful photographs guide you to success. Recipes are explained in a step-by-step manner and accompanied by tips for refined results.

Most of all, we wish to inspire you to create **Christmas with *Victoria*** your way, combining the traditions you cherish with new expressions of the season's true meaning. More than any other holiday, Christmas gives us a chance to renew friendships, to strengthen family ties, to revel in our memories, and to celebrate traditions.

From snow-lined streets gladdened by twinkling trees to the warmth of your own lovely home—and from the **Victoria** family to you—may this be the merriest of Christmases.

Editors of **Christmas with *Victoria***

Votive candles gleam through translucent jackets of metallic ribbon.

Chapter I

Decorations

Come home to the pure joy of Christmas traditions.
Revel in the glow of candles, the scents of
evergreen and roses, and the sparkle of silver
ornaments on the family tree.

Trimmed with photographs—from Victoria *editors' albums—that have been handcrafted into silvery keepsake ornaments, this tree displays Christmas traditions.*

O Christmas Tree

*Laden with decorations old and new, the tree stands green
and fragrant at the center of the family celebration.*

Christmas trees were already a holiday tradition in Prince Albert's native Germany when he married Britain's Queen Victoria in 1840. The Saxon custom became a worldwide sensation when the homesick prince imported small evergreen trees from his ancestral home to Windsor Castle during Christmas of 1841. To Albert's delight, the queen had the trees decorated with fruits, flowers, glass ornaments, and ribbons. On Christmas Eve, she lighted small candles amid the branches.

This first Victorian Christmas tree caught the fancy of courtiers and common people alike and became what is today an enduring symbol of the season.

Family Portrait Ornaments

Consider making two sets—one to keep and one to give, perhaps to welcome a bride or a groom into the family circle.

You will need: family photographs, purchased silver frames with hooks for hanging, velvet ribbon, and small labels.

1. Copy each photograph on a photocopier, enlarging or reducing to fit your choice of frame. You may wish

to make a color copy to duplicate the sepia tones of old photos.

2. Frame the copy—or the original if it fits and will not be damaged in the process—in a small silver frame. If your frame does not have a hook, attach a small hook purchased at a hardware store.

3. Loop a length of ribbon through the hook and tie it in a bow.

4. Attach a small label to the back of the frame, listing the name and the age of the person pictured and the date of the photograph if known.

The holly's up, the

house is all bright,

The tree is ready, the

candles alight:

Rejoice and be glad,

all children tonight!

—*P. Cornelius*

The Yule trees,

and the dreams

all children dream.

The tremulous glow

of candles in rows.

The gold and silver

of angels and globes.

And the splendor of

tinsel and toys

under trees.

—Boris Pasternak

Paper Cones

Fill these easy-to-fashion ornaments with party favors, candy, and other small gifts.

You will need: thick decorative or solid wrapping paper, ribbon or trim, holiday stickers or stamps, thick craft glue, clothespins, hole punch, ribbon for hanging, and tissue paper.

1. To make each cone, measure and cut a 6" square from the wrapping paper. Glue a 6" piece of ribbon or trim along the top edge. Use holiday stickers or stamps to trim solid paper.

2. Place the square facedown on a flat, clean surface. Holding the bottom right corner, roll the top right corner toward the bottom left corner, forming a cone.

Secure the cone with a dab of glue and let it dry, clamping with a clothespin until set.

3. Using a hole punch, make 2 holes in the cone on opposite sides of the top. For the hanger, insert a length of ribbon through the holes and knot the ends.

4. Fill the cone with tissue paper and a small surprise if desired.

Fabergé-Inspired Ornaments

Inspired by the elaborate designs of Fabergé, decoupage transforms plain wooden eggs into artful ornaments.

You will need: small wooden eggs; scraps of wrapping paper, cards, and magazines; decoupage glue; paintbrush; satin ribbon; and pins or tacks.

1. For each egg, clip small to midsize designs and motifs from wrapping paper, cards, and magazines.

2. Using a paintbrush, apply the glue to the back of each clipping; place each where desired on the egg. Smooth out any wrinkles with your fingertips. When the design is complete, brush a final coat of glue over the entire egg to seal the edges. Allow the glue to dry thoroughly.

3. To hang, press a pin or a tack through a small loop of satin ribbon and into the top of the egg.

Dozens of dazzling painted eggs and gilded stars consume the branches of this Christmas tree at New York's famous Russian Tea Room.

As you trim the tree, select a few special ornaments to display in a tabletop bowl. Tie a sprig of rosemary and a ribbon to each for the fragrant scent of remembrance.

Christmas has really begun when the boxes of trimmings (left) come down from the attic or up from the cellar. Each ornament has a story of its own—the giver of this one, the occasion for that—all souvenirs of happy times past. This year when Christmas is over and you're packing up the boxes, include the most meaningful holiday cards and notes you've received. When the boxes are opened next year, you will enjoy them all over again.

Christmas is here,

Merry old Christmas.

Gift-bearing,

heart-touching,

Joy-bringing Christmas,

Day of grand memories,

King of the year!

—Washington Irving

A Tree for Feathered Friends

Winter birds will welcome seed-covered wreaths and bells made with ingredients that are safe for them to eat.

You will need: flour; water; corn syrup; birdseed; bowl; rolling pin; waxed paper; drinking glass; knife; cranberries and holly berries; red, green, or violet raffia or twine; 2¼"-diameter peat pots for bells; paintbrush; and needle and thread.

1. For the **birdseed wreaths**, mix ¾ cup flour, ½ cup water, 3 tablespoons corn syrup, and 4 cups birdseed in a bowl. Roll the mixture flat on waxed paper. Using the glass, cut circles out of the birdseed mixture. Using a knife, cut a small hole in the center of each circle to form wreaths. Place the wreaths on a tray covered with waxed paper.

2. Decorate the wreaths with holly berries or cranberries. Let them dry for 4 to 6 hours. Then turn the wreaths over and let them dry for an additional 4 to 6 hours. For each wreath, wrap a length of raffia around the wreath and tie a bow at the top. For the hanger, tie a small loop of raffia or twine onto the bow.

3. For the **birdseed bells**, mix ¾ cup flour, ¼ cup water, and 3 tablespoons corn syrup in a bowl. Use a paintbrush to coat the peat pots with the syrup mixture. Roll the pots in the birdseed, completely covering the sides of the pots. Place the bells on waxed paper and let them dry for 4 to 6 hours.

4. To make a clapper for each bell, use a needle and thread to string 4 or 5 cranberries. Pass the needle through the top of the bell and knot the thread to secure the cranberry clapper. To make a loop for hanging each bell, thread a length of twine through the drainage hole of the pot and knot the twine at the top of the bell. Form a loop by knotting the twine again several inches from the top of the bell.

Decked with treats for your feathered friends, this tree is fun for the children to decorate.

Mantels Made Merry

Swags of greenery cloak the fireplace,
inviting the eye to linger.

❦

A Gifted Garland

This glorious cascade begins with a base of fresh Maine balsam.
To make your garland, gather boughs of the evergreens you prefer.

You will need: clippings of fresh evergreen and florist's wire (or a purchased evergreen garland), fresh rosebuds and dried flowers, glass florist's vials, dried leaves, gold spray paint, and tiny wrapped packages.

1. To make a swag from tree clippings, gather several small branches together and tightly wrap florist's wire around the branches to secure them. Continue wiring the branches together to form a garland. (Or purchase a garland to use. For fresh evergreen garlands, see Resources on page 140.) Be sure the garland is long enough to drape over the ends of the mantel and full enough for an abundant look.

2. To keep the rosebuds fresh, insert each bud into a glass florist's vial. Tuck the rose-filled vials and the dried flowers into the greenery.

3. For a hint of gold, gild dried leaves by spraying them with gold paint. Let them dry thoroughly and then set them in the greenery. Place small wrapped packages along the finished garland.

Crowned with materials in Christmas colors—red and white roses, golden leaves, and deep green branches—the hearth in this New Orleans French Quarter home awaits a candlelight tour.

The treasures that fill the house the rest of the year need not move to make room for Christmas. Leave them in place and fill in around them with greenery and seasonal embellishments. Surround a mantel clock with fresh lilies and evergreens, ribbons, and miniature musical instruments. Twine holly vines or cedar sprays and fresh roses under and around framed photographs (above).

Dried Hydrangea Garland

To emulate the polished design at right, attach roses, ribbon, and extra hydrangea blooms at the garland's center.

You will need: dried hydrangea blooms, florist's wire, fresh roses, wire-edged ribbon, and small tacks or hooks.

1. To make a rope of hydrangea, arrange the blooms so that the stems are together and the blooms overlap. The garland should be approximately twice the width of the mirror or the mantel.

2. Using florist's wire, tightly wrap the stems together. Wire a few extra blooms and roses to the center of the garland. Twist lengths of ribbon around the finished garland.

3. Drape the garland across the mantel or the mirror, securing it at the corners and the center with tacks or hooks.

Paper butterfly cutouts, attached with wire, complete the finished hydrangea garland draped across the mantel mirror.

A Candlelight Christmas

*The amber warmth
of a candle's flame draws
us to the table.*

The subtle elegance of a candle's flame inspires conversation and enhances the pleasures of dinner. Consider any of these classic ways to bring dining room candles to light: Ring tapers with a wreath for a glowing centerpiece, arrange a grouping of candlesticks on a mirrored plateau at the heart of the table, or light a trail of votive candles to mark places for the meal.

A bounty of greenery and seasonal fruits surrounds a quartet of candlesticks (above) embellished with golden tassels that match the tapers. Shimmering ribbon bows and sprigs of berries dress crystal candlesticks (left) for the season.

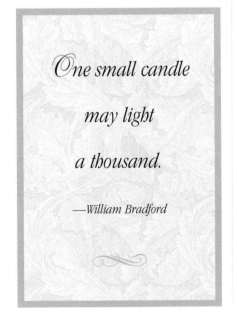

*One small candle

may light

a thousand.*

—William Bradford

Custom-make a set of beeswax tapers to the length and the width you prefer.

Beeswax Tapers

Sweet smelling and long lasting, beeswax candles have figured prominently for thousands of years in folklore and religion. Making them yourself is simple and satisfying.

You will need: honeycomb-patterned beeswax sheets, candlewicks, craft knife, and ruler.

1. For each candle, use the craft knife to trim the beeswax to the size you desire. One edge determines the candle's height, while the perpendicular edge determines its thickness. To make an 8" taper, cut the wax sheet to measure 8" x 12". For beeswax sheets, see Resources on page 140.

2. Cut a length of wick at least 1" longer than the height of the taper. Place the wick ¼" from the edge determining the height, with 1 end of the wick extending beyond the wax. Roll the edge over the wick, keeping the wick taut and pressing the wax against the wick to hold it in place.

3. Continue rolling evenly and fairly tightly until the candle is formed. Press the outside edge of the wax against the taper to secure it.

Terrific Tapers

As you roll the beeswax sheets into a stunning set of candles, experiment with these designs:

• *Make a votive by cutting a long, narrow beeswax strip and rolling it from the short edge.*

• *Make spiraled tapers by cutting a beeswax sheet in half diagonally, forming two triangles. Roll each triangle from its short edge to its tip.*

• *Create swirled tapers by stacking two beeswax triangles in contrasting colors. Offset the bottom edge of the top triangle about 1" above the bottom edge of the other triangle. Keep the short edges of the triangles aligned and roll the triangles together from their short edges to their tips.*

*Handcraft a **bay leaf-and-ribbon candle jacket** (top left) and a **bay leaf-and-lemon candle jacket** (bottom).*

Aglow in Silver and Gold

Prettiest in multiples, these ribbon-wrapped votive candles positively glow along a mantelpiece, a sideboard, or a coffee table.

You will need (for each candle holder): 2"-tall round clear glass votive candle holder, scrap of posterboard, 2"-wide wire-edged mesh ribbon in gold or silver, hot-glue gun and glue sticks, gold or silver wax finish, dried bay leaves and/or dried lemon slices, ¾ yard ⅛"-wide ribbon in gold and silver, and 3-mm gold or silver beads.

1. Measure the circumference of the candle holder and add ½". Cut a ½"-wide strip of posterboard and a length of wire mesh ribbon to this length.

2. Hot-glue the ends of the posterboard strip together to form a circle, overlapping the ends ¼". The circle should fit loosely around the candle holder.

3. Align 1 long end of the ribbon with the posterboard base and then glue to the base, overlapping and gluing the ends of the ribbon.

4. Following the manufacturer's directions, lightly apply gold or silver wax finish to the front of the bay leaves. Let them dry. For the **bay leaf-and-ribbon candle jacket**, glue the bay leaves on the mesh ribbon jacket as desired. Tie a 6-loop bow of ⅛" ribbon and glue it to the bay leaves. For the **bay leaf-and-lemon candle jacket,** cut a dried lemon slice in half; repeat for the number of halves needed to cover the jacket. Align the cut edge of each half with the bottom of the jacket; glue them in place. Overlap the ends of the bay leaves slightly and glue them to the bottom edge of the lemon slices.

5. If desired, glue beads around the top edge of the jacket. (For safety's sake, do not leave burning candles unattended.)

When Company Comes

As friends and family stay for Christmas, hospitality means welcoming those we love.

A guest room must never be an afterthought, but rather a place where welcome is a tangible presence. Extend your holiday decorating scheme into the guest room, tossing a tartan throw and red velvet pillows on the bed, hanging a garland and greeting cards around the doorway, and leaving a small gift on the bedside table.

The most accommodating hostess can anticipate a guest's needs by putting herself in his or her place and then providing whatever will make the visit most comfortable and enjoyable. Before guests arrive, freshen a seldom-used room with greenery, flowers, or potpourri. Guests will appreciate crisp linens, plenty of towels, an extra blanket, and an alarm clock.

Decorated for the season, guest rooms become a continuation of the the holiday celebration. At Stillington Hall, a Tudor-style inn in Massachusetts, bedrooms already rich with antiques are iced with pine, roses, and ribbons.

Rosemary, ivy, and germander topiaries are lavished with ribbons and fresh flowers to create a fragrant display.

Winter Wonders

Tabletop trees invite you to examine the glories of nature on an intimate scale.

opiaries in tole pots are so handsome that you'll want to keep them on the sideboard all winter long.

Cultivate living topiaries like these by pruning stems away from the base and the center of the plant, leaving only the top branches. Clip and round off the remaining branches and conceal the base with moss. Decorate the topiaries simply with flowers and ribbons. Dress rosemary (far left) with only a shining bow of bronze. Train globe ivy to grow in a sphere (center) and tuck fresh roses and preserved dogwood blossoms into the foliage. Color germander left (right) in violet with sprigs of lamb's ears, delphinium, and hydrangea. For a bit of topiary fantasy, weave myrtle sprigs with fresh herbs and flowers into a lush centerpiece (right) for Christmas dinner.

Herbs and Flowers Centerpiece

You will need: sprigs of myrtle, rue, and southernwood; florist's wire; florist's foam sphere and brick; terracotta pot; small branch; flowers of anise, hyssop, garlic chives, and calamint; and red roses.

1. Bind a few sprigs of myrtle with florist's wire. Insert the stems into the foam sphere. Repeat until the sphere is densely covered with myrtle.

2. Cut the foam brick to fit tightly inside the pot. Press the foam into the pot, filling to the rim.

3. Push the sphere onto the branch.

Push the other end of the branch firmly into the potted foam.

4. Decorate the sphere and conceal the base with myrtle, roses, other flowers, and greenery.

A tower of fruits and gilded pinecones becomes doubly impressive when placed in front of a mirror.

A Fruitful Tower

Stack crystal cake pedestals to shape a "tree" of fruits, herbs, and spices.

You will need: 3 cake pedestals, ranging from small to large; masking tape; small candlestick; pinecones; pomegranates; gold spray paint; citrus fruits; whole cloves; Seckel pears; sprigs of various herbs and greenery; and gold dressmaker's bullion.

1. Stack the cake pedestals from large to small, securing them at their bases with tape. Place the candlestick in the middle of the top pedestal and secure it with tape. Lightly spray the pinecones and the pomegranates with gold paint and let them dry.

2. To make each pomander, peel away vertical or horizontal strips of the outer skin of a citrus fruit. Stud the exposed strips with whole cloves. Save the prettiest pomander for the top and rest it upon the candlestick.

3. Carefully fill in the spaces between the pedestals with fruits, pomanders, pinecones, and pomegranates. Then tuck in sprigs of herbs and greenery. Drape the tower with strands of dressmaker's bullion. (For dressmaker's bullion, see Resources on page 140.)

Tiny Trees and Lights

Place handmade topiaries and votive lights in leaf-covered terra-cotta pots. Set next to a rosemary standard, they animate a tabletop.

You will need: small terra-cotta pots, fresh or dried bay leaves, spray adhesive or hot-glue gun and glue sticks, sheet moss, small foam sphere, U-shaped florist's pins, sprigs of rosemary, household paraffin or beeswax for votive candles, and candlewicks.

1. Cover each pot with fresh or dried bay leaves. Beginning at the rim and working downward in overlapping rows, attach the leaves with spray adhesive or hot glue. Fold the points of the leaves over the rim of the pot. Leave the bottom of the pot uncovered so that it will stand upright.

2. For the **moss topiary**, completely cover a foam sphere with moss, using U-shaped florist's pins or glue. Balance the sphere on the pot rim. For a **miniature rosemary tree**, tuck several sprigs of rosemary tightly into a pot.

3. For a **votive light**, fill a terra-cotta pot with melted household paraffin or beeswax and a wick. Or set a purchased votive candle inside the pot.

A holiday tablescape details the effervescent colors and lilylike blooms of amaryllis. The selections used here include miniature Salmon Pearl, vivid Scarlet Baby, peachy Amourette, and red-and-white striped Clown.

Love in Bloom

Spring bulbs, rushed into Christmas flowers,
gladden the winter heart.

*T*hough they naturally flower in spring, amaryllis, hyacinths, and paper-whites are most agreeable to earlier arrival. The simple (and nearly foolproof) process of forcing these bulbs yields fragrant rewards. Display the forced blooms in the center of a coffee table, on a sideboard, or in a breakfast room window. A basket of bulbs and the materials for forcing them make a splendid gift, especially when presented early enough for the recipient to time the blooms for Christmas Day.

Whether you give bulbs away or keep them to grow yourself, it's important to buy bulbs that have been pretreated for forcing and to follow the instructions below for each type of flower.

Amaryllis

For each bulb, plant the bulb in a 6"- or 8"-diameter clay pot so that the top half of the bulb is exposed. Water thoroughly and then keep the soil fairly dry until shoots appear. Afterward, water when the soil feels dry to the touch. Move the pot to a warm, sunny spot. As the stalk develops, you may need to insert a stake to support it. If you are planning to use amaryllis for a particular occasion, plant the bulbs about 6 weeks before you want them to bloom. Amaryllis will remain in bloom for 2 to 8 weeks.

In the depth of winter, I finally learned that inside me

there lay an invincible summer. —*Albert Camus*

Growing in vases that are modern copies of eighteenth-century originals, forced hyacinths are a sweet-smelling pleasure.

Mass several paperwhite bulbs in a single container for mounds of fragrant flowers.

Hyacinths

Popular during Victorian and Edwardian times, hyacinth vases cradle bulbs in their cups while allowing the roots to trail below. You can find antique hyacinth vases or replicas in gardening shops, or see Resources on page 140. You may grow hyacinth in such a vase or in potting soil, following the directions for paperwhites.

To use a vase, fill with water and set a hyacinth bulb in the opening. Maintain a water level just below the bottom of the bulb. Place the container in a cool, dark spot until the bulb has developed leaves and roots; then move it to a warm, sunny place. Hyacinth blooms, pleasantly perfumed, will stay fresh for 3 to 6 weeks.

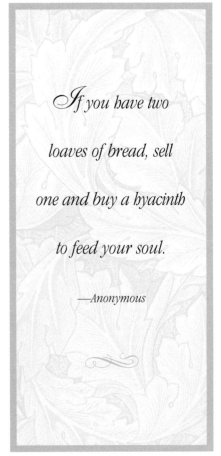

If you have two loaves of bread, sell one and buy a hyacinth to feed your soul.

—*Anonymous*

Paperwhites

Select a shallow, plastic-lined container and fill it with pebbles. Bury the bulbs halfway in the pebbles and maintain a layer of water just below the bottom of the bulbs. Or select a container at least twice as tall as the bulbs and plant the bulbs ½" apart in potting soil with the tops exposed. Water whenever the soil feels dry to the touch.

Place the container in a cool, dark spot. When the bulbs develop roots and leaves, move them to a warm, sunny spot. Paperwhites will bloom—and fill the entire house with their fragrance—for 3 to 6 weeks.

Retaining their shape and color as they dry, flowers like globe amaranth, roses, and celosia are ideal for this everlasting wreath.

Wreaths All Around

*In each charmed circle, there is a sign of greeting
and the embrace of nature's goodness.*

At Christmastime, rings of evergreen boughs and dried flowers hold up beautifully outdoors, while delicate fresh flowers bring the joy inside.

An Everlasting Wreath

Flowers and herbs that hold their shape and color as they dry are called everlastings and are available year-round in florist's shops and crafts stores. To use everlastings from your own garden, you must snip them at the peak of bloom.

You will need: everlastings like globe amaranth, roses, seedpods, celosia, artemisia, Mexican sage, bay leaves, and rosemary; twine; florist's wire; purchased vine wreath or lengths of vinelike wisteria, honeysuckle, or grapevine; and a flat-head screwdriver.

1. To dry the everlastings, strip the stalks of all but the topmost leaves and bundle the cuttings with twine or florist's wire. Hang them upside down in a dry place for about 3 weeks.

2. Weave lengths of vine into a circle to serve as a base for the dried materials. Choose vines in lengths to equal 8 times the desired diameter of your finished wreath. Tie a length of vine in a loose knot to form the wreath's diameter and then wrap the loose ends around the circular base, tucking the ends into the wreath. Weave additional lengths of vine around the base until it is as thick as you like. (If necessary, use a screwdriver to wedge the vine ends into the wreath.)

3. Tuck the ends of each bundle of flowers and herbs into the vine wreath base, securing the bundle with florist's wire. Continue until the vine wreath is completely covered. Use your screwdriver to pry apart the vines as needed to insert the dried materials.

A ring of Fraser and dried larkspur holds paperwhite bulbs, ideal for winter blooming.

Heap the holly! / Wreath the pine! / Train the dainty Christmas vine—

Let the breadth of fir and bay / Mingle on the festal day. —Helen Chase

Many Christmas tree farms provide fresh wreaths or evergreen clippings from the trees. To fashion clippings into a wreath, attach them with florist's wire to a wire wreath base, available at crafts and florist's shops. Use enough clippings for a full, lush wreath and embellish with the trimmings of your choosing: fresh or dried flowers and fruits, ribbon or cord, tiny ornaments, or clusters of holly berries.

Larkspur-Flocked Fraser

Larkspur's delicate white blooms resemble a dusting of snow on this evergreen wreath. If you prefer, approximate the effect with tallow berries instead.

You will need: purchased Fraser fir wreath, sprigs of dried larkspur, florist's wire, paperwhite bulbs, and white organdy ribbon.

1. Secure sprigs of larkspur around the wreath with short lengths of florist's wire. (For a fresh evergreen wreath, see Resources on page 140.)

2. Nestle a cluster of paperwhite bulbs at the bottom of the wreath. Slip wire through the base of each bulb and attach to the wreath. After Christmas remove the bulbs and force their blooms (see page 37).

3. Tie a ribbon bow and attach it to the wreath above the bulbs.

Fresh flowers add color and fragrance to a traditional green wreath hanging at a window. To duplicate it, wire bundles of blooms and greenery to a vine wreath base and adorn it with a bow made of silky golden cord.

Centerpiece Wreath

Let your wassail bowl serve as a centerpiece as well as refreshment. Set the punch bowl in the center of an evergreen wreath and then tuck freesia blooms, red roses, or berries around the wreath.

A covered porch shelters a cozy wicker settee adorned for the holidays. Evergreen and berries trim the back of the settee while red plaid flannel pillows cushion the effect.

A Lasting First Impression

Call out a jolly greeting from the front porch, the lamppost, and the garden gate.

Everyone who passes by will know you are celebrating Christmas when your attention to detail extends to the outdoors.

Dress post lanterns (right) and porch lights with bows and greenery. Window boxes, normally barren this time of year, can brim with magnolia leaves, nandina berries, and boxwood. If your winters are mild, welcome guests at the garden gate (below) with a bouquet of tulips, paperwhites, stars-of-Bethlehem, and bleached honeysuckle vine tied together with raffia. Secure the fresh flowers in water-filled florist's vials to keep them fresh for days.

Consider the climate when choosing materials that will be exposed to the elements. A covered porch (left) may shelter decorations like an antique sled and ice skates. Let the children collect pinecones, evergreen, and lady apples for a seasonal basket set near the door.

The Freshest Arrangements

To prepare greenery for use outdoors or inside, cut stems at an angle and soak them in tepid water overnight in a cool place.

Freshen ivy, boxwood, juniper, pine, arborvitae, and fir by submerging whole stems in warm water for 1 hour. Arrangements placed in direct sun will likely require weekly misting with water or a floral preservative.

Create packages so exquisite they become gifts in themselves.

Chapter II

Gifts

Our collection of handmade gift ideas for the home
and from the kitchen offers something for everyone
on your Christmas list.

Hearts will delight in seeing a room full of presents wrapped in red and gold.

An Elegant Presentation

❧

A beautiful wrapping doubles the delight of every gift.

Friends and family will treasure gifts packaged with your personal touch. And you'll enjoy giving unique presents made with extra love and care. Completed with luxurious ribbons, topped with adorable ornaments, or handmade with fine fabrics, the wrapping is as special as the gift inside.

Tiny packages topped with artist Margaret Furlong's golden shell ornaments make a magical display under the Christmas tree.

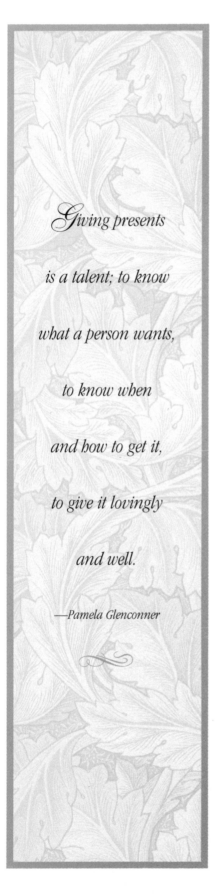

Giving presents

is a talent; to know

what a person wants,

to know when

and how to get it,

to give it lovingly

and well.

—Pamela Glenconner

❧

A soft velvet bag hints at the smoothness of a bottle of fine wine or favorite spirits.

Wrapped in holly red fabric bags, a host of Christmas favors brings holiday cheer.

$\mathcal{S}$ecured with gold or silver cords or with slender ropes of velvet cording, beautiful fabric bags will be as welcome as the presents they hold.

Velvet Wine-Bottle Wraps

Stitch together two rectangles of velvet for a stylish wrapping your friends will love.

You will need (for 1 bag): ½ yard 40"-wide velvet or other festive fabric, thread to match, and ¾ yard satin cording with tassels.

1. All seam allowances are ½".

2. From the fabric, cut 2 (7" x 23") pieces. With the right sides facing and the raw edges aligned, stitch the pieces together along three sides, leaving 1 short end open for the top.

3. For the top hem, turn under ⅝" and stitch ½" from the folded edge. Trim the seams, clip the corners, and turn the bag right side out. Fold 4" to 5" of the top edge to the inside of the bag.

4. Insert the wine bottle, adjusting the top edge of the bag as necessary. Tie the cording around the neck of the bottle to secure.

$\mathcal{F}$itting $\mathcal{F}$abric

Any bottled gift—be it bath oil, flavored vinegar, or homemade liqueur—is enhanced by a fabric gift bag. When selecting fabric, let the recipient and the gift be your guide.

• Jewel-toned velvet or rich tapestry is lovely for a gift of wine or spirits.

• If your friend prefers a more casual style, try a flannel tartan in Christmas colors secured with twine.

• Gifts from the kitchen pair perfectly with checked fabrics secured with grosgrain ribbon or in bags made from crisp linen.

• Use handkerchief linen or soft brocade cinched with satin or organdy ribbon to hold a bottle of bath oil.

Edge cozy flannel pillowcases with a message your friends will adore.

A Merry Message

Handstitch personal presents worth more than words can say.

Noel Pillowcases

You may want to use extra cording to spell out greetings on blankets, throw pillows, or towels.

You will need (for 1 standard pillowcase): flannel pillowcase, transfer pen or pencil, 1½ yards ⅛" twisted silk cording, tape, clear thread, and needle.

1. Wash the pillowcase according to the manufacturer's instructions. On a flat surface and using a transfer pen or pencil, write "Noel" as desired across the open edge of the pillowcase, creating a pattern. Use a transfer pen on a dark-colored pillowcase and a transfer pencil on a light-colored pillowcase.

2. To attach the cording, tape the ends of the cording to prevent fraying. Double-thread the needle with the clear thread. Stitch 1 end of the cording to the left end of the pattern on the pillowcase, securing the cording with several stitches. Whipstitch the cording to the pattern, following the natural direction of the cording. Secure the cording end with several stitches. Remove the tape and trim any frayed ends or excess.

3. To care for the pillowcase, wash it in cold water on the delicate cycle and hang it to dry. To iron, turn the case inside out and use a warm, not hot, setting.

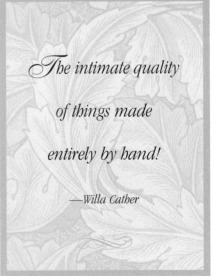

The intimate quality of things made entirely by hand!

—*Willa Cather*

Wild rose, grape, and cedar leaves are pressed into purchased candles and then coated with a thin layer of paraffin. The result is a trio with subtle, natural beauty.

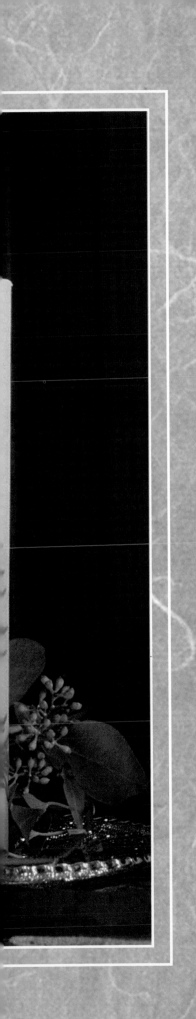

Botanical Gifts

*Let nature lead the way
to enchanting gifts.*

Leaf-Printed Pillars

*Adorn candles with a variety
of leaf shapes and shades for a present
that's both personal and practical.*

You will need (for 3 candles): aluminum foil; 1 (16-ounce) package household paraffin; empty, clean aluminum coffee can; dried leaves; 3 plain purchased pillar candles; metal spoon; and pliers.

1. Cover your work surface with foil. Melt the paraffin in a double boiler over medium heat. (To make a double boiler, place the coffee can in a pan of water on the stove. Put the paraffin in the coffee can.)

2. For each candle, position the leaves as desired on the candle. Heat the back of the spoon in the pan of water or over a stove burner. Use the heated back of the spoon to gently press the leaves into the candle wax, pressing all edges of the leaves. (The heated spoon will melt the candle wax beneath the leaves, allowing them to recess into the wax.)

3. For each candle, use the pliers to hold the candle by the wick and dip the entire candle into the melted paraffin. Quickly and carefully remove the candle from the paraffin to the covered work surface. Allow the layer of paraffin to cool. For tall candles, dip the bottom half of the candle into the melted paraffin. Quickly remove the candle and allow the paraffin to cool. With your fingertips, hold the candle from the bottom and dip the top half of the candle into the melted paraffin. Quickly remove the candle and allow the paraffin to cool.

4. Gently smooth any rough, uneven places on the candle with a sponge or with your fingertips.

Forest Pins

Slender twigs frame delicate fronds, forming gift pins to be worn singly or in a cluster. Harvest the greenery from your yard or sun-room. Begin this project at least a week in advance to allow time for the fern to dry before assembling.

You will need (for 1 pin): fern frond tip, about ¾" to 1¼" long; paper towels; large book; scrap of cardboard; scrap of parchment paper; scrap of cream textured paper; craft glue; toothpick; greenery clippers; small twigs, no larger than ⅜" in diameter; hot-glue gun and glue sticks; and a 1½" metal pin back.

1. Place the fern tip between paper towels to remove any moisture. Then press the fern tip between the pages of a large book or a phone directory. Weight it with a heavy object for approximately one week.

2. From the cardboard scrap, cut a small square or rectangle approximately ¼" larger on all sides than the fern. Cut the same size piece from the parchment and textured papers. With the edges aligned, glue the parchment piece to the back of the cardboard and the textured piece to the front.

3. Using a toothpick, apply the craft glue to the back of the fern. Then center and glue the fern to the front of the cardboard.

4. Use the clippers to cut the twigs into four pieces to fit around the edges of the cardboard. Hot-glue the twigs to the edges of the cardboard. Cut 4 more twig pieces for a second row and then hot-glue them to the inside of the first row of twigs.

5. Hot-glue the pin back to the back of the cardboard and let dry completely.

Old family photos become gifts to treasure when they're artfully framed with ivy leaves, berries, and twigs.

For an extra holiday touch, gild the terra-cotta pots with a shimmering gold or silver wax finish.

Petite Pot Ornaments

Miniature terra-cotta pots become charming gifts when crowned with dried roses or pomegranates.

You will need (for each): 2" terra-cotta pot; florist's foam brick; knife; 8" piece raffia for hanger; U-shaped florist's pin; 3 small dried roses and tiny dried leaf stems for rose pot; sheet moss; hot-glue gun and glue sticks; half a florist's pick; and a small dried pomegranate for pomegranate pot.

1. Fill the pot with florist's foam by placing the pot facedown on the foam brick and gently pressing down until the pot is filled with the foam. Using a knife, slice off the foam level with the top of the pot.

2. **For the rose pot,** press the roses into the foam, leaving a small space in the center. For the hanger, fold the raffia in half and knot the ends together. Using a florist's pin, press the knotted end of the raffia into the foam at the center of the pot. Press the leaf stems into the foam, filling in around the roses and the hanger.

3. **For the pomegranate pot,** tear off a patch of moss equal in size to the pot top. Glue the moss to the foam. Glue the florist's pick half to the base of the pomegranate and let it dry. Press the pick into the center of the moss and hot-glue around the edges to secure. Fold the raffia in half and knot the center around the tip of the pomegranate. Tie the loose ends in a bow.

Bright dried roses peek above the rim of this petite pot ornament.

All the

peace

which springs

From the

large aggregate

of little things.

—Hannah More

Violet Bouquet Ornament

Tie together dozens of tiny blooms for a brilliant bouquet friends will love adding to their Christmas tree.

You will need (for 1 bouquet): 4 dozen silk violets with 5" stems, 5 silk leaves with wire stems, florist's tape, and sheer ribbon.

1. Tape the violet blooms together. Handling all the flowers as 1 unit, evenly arrange the leaves with the right sides facing toward the flowers. Handling the flowers and the leaves as 1 unit, wrap the tape around the center of the stems.

2. Tie the ribbon into a bow over the tape. Tie the bouquet on the tree among the ornaments.

*Tiny colorful violets tied on the tree
bring a burst of springtime color.*

A sculptural effect is achieved with rows of dried flowers, metallic ribbons, and seedpods.

Pomanders

*These festive gifts bear a
spice-rich incense.*

Filigreed balls of gold or silver filled with rare spices, pomanders were medieval charms for preventing illness. Today, pomanders made from clove-studded fruit are a beloved Christmas tradition. Take a clever approach and make a foam-based pomander scented with oil.

Artful Pomander

*For long-lived results, fashion
a stylish pomander from a florist's
foam base. After a few months,
refresh the aroma with drops
of essential oil.*

You will need (for 1 pomander): small foam sphere; sheet moss; U-shaped florist's pins; craft glue; small terra-cotta pot; bay leaves; nuts; dried flowers such as strawflowers, gomphrena, and seedpods; ⅛"-wide ribbon; and essential oil.

1. Using florist's pins or glue, cover the foam sphere with pieces of sheet moss.

2. Cover the pot with bay leaves (see Tiny Trees and Lights on page 33). Glue the moss-covered sphere to the rim of the pot and then glue nuts, flowers, and ⅛"-wide ribbon to the sphere in an all-around design or in rows.

*Studded with nuts, a moss-covered globe rests among
traditional fruit pomanders, imparting spirited scents.*

3. Scent the pomander with 3 to 4 drops of essential oil.

Fresh Fruit Pomander

*An ideal project for children, this
traditional pomander is studded with
cloves and rolled in spices.*

You will need (for 1 pomander): powdered orrisroot; ground allspice, cloves, or cinnamon; essential oil; firm orange, apple, or pear; whole cloves; and ½"-wide ribbon.

1. Mix together equal parts of the powdered orrisroot and ground spice. Add ½ teaspoon of essential oil to the spice mixture.

2. Stud the fruit with the whole cloves by making a linear pattern or by covering completely. If you are using an orange, you may need to use a toothpick to pierce the rind before inserting the cloves. If you plan to hang the pomander from a ribbon, leave a ½" path uncovered around the center of the fruit. (This will form a groove to hold the ribbon.)

3. Roll the clove-studded fruit in the spice mixture. Gently tap the fruit to remove the excess mixture.

4. To make a hanger, tie the ribbon around the fruit along the uncovered ½" path. Knot the ribbon ends together to form a loop for hanging.

Herbs from the Heart

Preserve the sights and the scents of the summer garden for inspiring holiday gifts.

Present a collection of herbs at Christmas, and your gift will be enjoyed throughout the winter as the leafy clusters bestow their signature scents.

A Graceful Swag

For wintertime enjoyment, hang this herbal swag next to the mantel and clip off bundles to toss into the fire.

You will need: 3 purchased dried pomegranates; power drill with ⅛" bit; 2½ yards of jute string or twine; fresh-cut fragrant herbs such as artemisia, oregano, rosemary, sage, scented geranium, and thyme; fresh-cut flowers or blooming herbs such as lamb's ears, marigolds, and Mexican sage; and a large-eyed tapestry needle.

1. Drill a hole from the top to the bottom through the center of each pomegranate. Set them aside. Cut 4 (6") lengths of jute string or twine. Set them aside.

2. Gather herbs and flowers into a 2½" diameter bundle. Wrap with 1 (6") length of string to secure. Trim the ends of the string close to the knot. Repeat to make 3 more bundles.

3. Cut 1½ yards of string. Thread the needle with a doubled strand of string and knot 1 end. Thread the pomegranates on the string, leaving 5" at the knotted end below the bottom pomegranate and 5" above the top pomegranate.

4. Insert the herb bundles between the doubled strands of string below, between, and on top of the pomegranates. Pull the free ends of the string to tighten. Tie a knot above the top bundle to secure. Knot the ends of the string together to make the hanger.

5. To scent your fire, clip 1 herb bundle and toss into the fire. Secure the remaining bundles with a knot. Save the pomegranates for another use; do not place them in the fire.

Meaningful Bouquets

A long-ago form of expression, flowers were thought to have specific meanings. This season, offer an arrangement of glad tidings with these blooms:

Baby's breath	*Constancy*	Myrtle	*Hopeful love*
Camellia	*Destiny*	Pansy	*Thoughts*
Evening primrose	*Sweet memories*	Parsley	*Entertaining*
Fern	*Fascination*	Rose	*Love*
Globe amaranth	*Unchangeable*	Rosemary	*Remembrance*
Holly	*Good wishes*	Sage	*Esteem*
Ivy	*Devotion*	Star-of-Bethlehem	*Reconciliation*
Larkspur	*Ardent attachment*	Statice	*Sympathy*

Blue-green Mexican sage, ruby red pomegranates, and pine-scented rosemary form a colorful swag that will last throughout the winter.

For the herb-lover, give the sweet aroma of fresh herbs fashioned in a long-lasting wreath.

A Living Herb Wreath

A well-watered wreath of fresh herbs will be enjoyed into the new year.

You will need: wreath-shaped florist's foam or several florist's foam bricks; plastic-coated chicken wire (to avoid rust); large plastic sheet (to protect the work surface); florist's wire; large plastic bag; U-shaped florist's pins; sprigs of fresh herbs such as purple basil, lavender, rosemary, sage, rue, mint, lamb's ears, and myrtle; and wire-edged ribbon.

1. Soak the florist's foam in water until completely wet. Cut a strip of chicken wire long enough to form the desired wreath shape.

2. Place the foam on the plastic sheet. If you are using the foam bricks, position several bricks to form a wreath. Wrap the chicken wire firmly around the florist's foam wreath or bricks, securing with florist's wire.

3. Cut the plastic bag so that it will open and lay flat. Cover the back side of the wreath with the bag, pinning the bag edges to the foam, using U-shaped florist's pins. (When you hang the wreath, the plastic covering behind the wreath will protect the wall from the wet florist's foam.)

4. To cover the wreath with herbs, bunch several herb sprigs together and wrap the stems with florist's wire. Insert the wire-wrapped stems of the herb tuft into the wet florist's foam. Continue until the wreath is completely covered with the herbs.

5. To attach a ribbon and bow to the wreath, push the U-shaped florist's pins through the ribbon and into the foam base where desired.

6. You may hang the wreath outside in warmer climates, but it must remain inside in areas where temperatures drop below freezing. To keep the living wreath fresh, regularly spray the base of the herbs with water, wetting the florist's foam.

Give your gift from the kitchen a handmade finish. Wrap a kraft paper circle over the lid and secure it with jute string or ribbon. Use sealing wax and a metal stamp to secure the string in style. Be sure to attach a decorative tag, offering hints for storing and enjoying your gift.

Gifts of Food: Sauces and Spices

*Collect assorted jars to fill with these flavorful condiments,
and you will have lovely gifts for everyone.*

Sherry-Apricot Mustard

Try this savory spread on pork tenderloin or on a sandwich made with slices of the Christmas ham. Package it in a glass container to show off its pretty color.

½ cup cream sherry
⅓ cup honey
¼ cup lemon juice
1 (6-ounce) package dried apricots
1 cup Dijon mustard

1. Combine the first 4 ingredients in a medium saucepan; stir well. Bring them to a boil and cook, stirring constantly, until the honey melts. Cover; reduce the heat and simmer for 15 minutes. Uncover and simmer for an additional 15 minutes, stirring occasionally. Remove from the heat and cool.
2. Position the knife blade in a food processor bowl. Transfer the apricot mixture to the processor bowl. Process the mixture until smooth. Transfer the mixture to a medium bowl; stir in the Dijon mustard. Store in glass containers in the refrigerator. Serve with pork.

Yield: 2 cups.

Rémoulade Sauce

Made mostly with pantry staples, this sauce is a delectable sandwich spread as well as a classic sauce for shellfish.

1 cup mayonnaise
⅓ cup thick, spicy steak sauce
3 tablespoons minced fresh cilantro or parsley
2 tablespoons minced fresh chives
2 tablespoons capers, drained
2 tablespoons sweet pickle relish, drained
1 tablespoon prepared mustard
¼ to ½ teaspoon hot sauce

Combine all the ingredients in a medium bowl; stir well. Store in glass containers in the refrigerator. Serve with seafood, roast beef, or turkey, or use as a sandwich spread.

Yield: 1¾ cups.

Cranberry-Kumquat Sauce

Tangy cranberries and fiery jalapeños meet a sweet counterpoint in kumquats. You'll find that the kumquat's skin is sweet tasting while its pulp is tart.

2 cups fresh or frozen cranberries
6 kumquats or 1 small orange, peeled
2 jalapeño peppers, seeded and finely chopped
3 tablespoons minced crystallized ginger
¾ cup sugar
¼ cup minced fresh mint

1. Position the slicing disc in a food processor bowl. With the processor running, press the cranberries through the food chute with the food pusher, using light pressure. Transfer the cranberries to a small bowl.
2. Coarsely chop the kumquats. Position the knife blade in the processor bowl. Add the kumquats, the peppers, and the ginger. Pulse 3 to 5 times or until the mixture is finely chopped; then add to the cranberries. Stir in the sugar and the mint. Store in glass containers in the refrigerator. Serve with pork or poultry.

Yield: 2 cups.

Of Course You Can

Canning extends the shelf life of homemade foods, allowing the giver to prepare some of her gifts long before the Christmas bustle begins. The process actually is quite simple: Food is packed into sterilized jars, topped with sterilized lids, and then submerged in boiling water for a specified time.

• Though metal bands can be safely reused, always use new lids to ensure a proper seal. Follow the manufacturer's directions for preparing the lids. Wash the jars, the bands, and the lids with hot, soapy water. Keep them hot in the dishwasher or in a sink filled with hot water.

• If you are using a stockpot or Dutch oven, fold a kitchen towel and place it in the bottom of the pot. Fill the pot halfway with water and bring to a boil.

• If the recipe's processing time is less than 10 minutes, sterilize the jars first by boiling them in water for 10 minutes. Remove the jars and fill them immediately, using a widemouthed funnel and following the recipe instructions for leaving space at the top of the jars. Run a rubber spatula between the food and the inside of the jar to remove any air bubbles. Wipe the jar rims with a clean, damp cloth, removing all traces of the food. Place the lids on the jar rims and screw the bands on tight.

• Place the filled jars in the boiling water. Position the jars 1" apart; water should be 1" to 2" above the lids. When the water returns to a boil, cover the pot and set a timer for the recommended processing time.

• Remove the jars and let them cool at room temperature for 12 to 24 hours. Check to see that each lid is concave, with a downward curve you can feel. Refrigerate any jars with faulty seals; store the properly sealed jars in a cool, dry place.

Raisin-Date Chutney

Let the flavors in this savory condiment mingle at room temperature for at least two weeks before presenting it as a gift.

2   oranges
4   cups sugar
5½ cups cider vinegar (5% acidity)
1½ teaspoons dried crushed red pepper
1   pound pitted dates, chopped
2   medium onions, chopped
2½ cups raisins

1. Grate the rind from the oranges; set the rind aside. Peel and discard the pith from the oranges. Chop the orange sections, discarding the seeds.
2. Combine the sugar, the vinegar, and the crushed red pepper in a large Dutch oven. Cook over low heat, stirring constantly, until the sugar dissolves. Add the chopped orange, the dates, the onion, the raisins, and half of the grated orange rind to the Dutch oven. Bring to a boil; reduce the heat and simmer uncovered for 2 hours or until the mixture is very thick, stirring occasionally. Remove from the heat and stir in the remaining orange rind.
3. Spoon the hot chutney into hot jars, filling to within ½" of the top. Remove the air bubbles and wipe the jar rims. Cover at once with the metal lids and screw on the bands. Process the jars in a boiling-water bath for 10 minutes. Let the chutney stand at room temperature for at least 2 weeks before serving. Refrigerate after opening.

    Yield: 7 half-pints.

Bittersweet Mint-Chocolate Sauce

On a gift tag, suggest serving the sauce warm over ice cream. But rest assured that the chocolate-lover on your list will invent plenty of ways to enjoy this treat.

2   (4.67-ounce) packages chocolate-covered mint wafer candies
2   (1-ounce) squares unsweetened chocolate
¾   cup whipping cream
1   teaspoon vanilla extract

Combine the first 3 ingredients in the top of a double boiler; bring the water to a boil. Reduce the heat to low; cook, stirring constantly, until smooth. Remove from the heat; stir in the vanilla. Serve the sauce warm. The sauce will keep in the refrigerator for up to 2 weeks.

Yield: about 1¾ cups.

The golden color of **Orange-White Chocolate Sauce** *hints at its light flavor.*

Orange-White Chocolate Sauce

Orange juice and zest are blended with white chocolate in a dessert sauce best served at room temperature, perhaps over a slice of warm pound cake.

3   (2-ounce) white chocolate-flavored baking bars
½   cup light corn syrup
¼   teaspoon grated orange rind
2   tablespoons fresh orange juice

1. Combine the first 3 ingredients in the top a double boiler; bring the water to a boil. Reduce the heat to low; cook until the chocolate melts, stirring frequently.
2. Gradually add the orange juice, stirring until smooth. Serve the sauce at room temperature. The sauce will keep in the refrigerator for up to 2 weeks.

Yield: 1¼ cups.

Stamps

Whether given singly or in sets, food gifts should look as good as they taste. With decorative stamps and textured paper, create elegant gift tags to label your gifts and to give storing and serving suggestions. For stamps, see Resources on page 140.

Merry
Christmas
Melanie

Apple Spice
Blend

Merry
Christmas!
Leslie

Small square spice jars hold a full measure of seasoning mixes. Label each jar with a handmade gift tag.

Taste
of
Tuscany

Give spice blends liberally as tokens of appreciation and personal remembrance. Buy whole spices and jars in bulk. Tie tags to each gift, listing tips for using the blends.

Apple Spice Blend

For a taste of Christmas, stir this mixture into applesauce, oatmeal, or pancake batter.

12 (3") sticks cinnamon
8 whole cloves
3 whole nutmegs
1 teaspoon whole allspice

1. Place all the ingredients in a mini food processor or a coffee grinder. Process until finely ground.
Yield: ½ cup.

2. For a terrific topping: combine equal parts Apple Spice Blend and sugar. Sprinkle over sugar-cookie dough before baking or over buttered bread before toasting.

Taste of Tuscany

Sprinkle this old-world blend over new potatoes or other fresh vegetables.

¼ cup dried sage
¼ cup dried rosemary
1 teaspoon salt
½ teaspoon black peppercorns

1. Place all the ingredients in a mini food processor or a coffee grinder. Process until finely ground.
Yield: ½ cup.

2. For savory roasted potatoes, coat 1 pound new potatoes with olive oil. Add 1 teaspoon kosher salt, 1 teaspoon Taste of Tuscany, and 1 clove garlic, crushed. Toss gently. Bake the potatoes at 400° for 30 minutes or until tender and lightly browned.

Wild Game Mix

Fennel seed gives this combination a licorice flavor. Use it as a base for a distinctive marinade.

2 tablespoons dried thyme
1 tablespoon black peppercorns
2 teaspoons fennel seeds
16 juniper berries
3 bay leaves

1. Place all the ingredients in a mini food processor or a coffee grinder. Process until the mixture is a fine powder.
Yield: approximately ⅓ cup.

2. For venison marinade, combine ½ cup dry red wine, 2 tablespoons olive oil, 1½ tablespoons Worcestershire sauce, and 1 teaspoon Wild Game Mix. Pour over 6 (4- to 6-ounce) bacon-wrapped venison fillets. Cover and marinate in the refrigerator for at least 8 hours.

Classic French Flavors

Ideal for making vinaigrette, this French mix is also a flavorful addition to grilled fish or chicken.

12 bay leaves
¼ cup dried thyme
¼ cup dried parsley flakes
2 tablespoons dried tarragon
2 tablespoons dried basil
1 teaspoon black peppercorns
1 teaspoon dried lemon peel

1. Place all the ingredients in a mini food processor or coffee grinder. Process until finely ground.
Yield: ⅓ cup.

2. For classic French vinaigrette, combine ⅔ cup olive oil, ⅓ cup red wine vinegar, 1 tablespoon Dijon mustard, 2 teaspoons Classic French Flavors, ¼ teaspoon salt, ¼ teaspoon sugar, and 1 clove garlic, crushed, in a jar. Cover the jar tightly and shake it vigorously.
Yield: 1 cup.

Arrange truffles in a papier-mâché box lined with crinkly handmade paper. Top the box with a shiny ribbon bow.

Gifts of Food: Sweet Surprises

Indulge friends with gifts they love best—
confections of chocolate, caramel, and coconut.

Strawberry-Chocolate Truffles

Making candy is as simple—
and rewarding—as baking.
The primary rule for both disciplines:
Begin with the best-quality
ingredients. Here, premium milk
chocolate makes the taste of these
truffles most memorable.

1   (10-ounce) package frozen
       sweetened strawberries, thawed
¾   cup whipping cream
4   (6-ounce) bars premium milk
       chocolate, coarsely chopped
1½ teaspoons vanilla extract
½   cup finely chopped almonds,
       toasted

1. Place the strawberries in a container of an electric blender; cover and process until smooth, stopping once to scrape down the sides. Pour the strawberry puree into a saucepan; bring to a boil over medium-high heat. Boil 20 to 25 minutes or until reduced to ¼ cup, stirring frequently. Stir in the whipping cream; bring to a boil. Remove from the heat; let cool slightly.

2. Place the chocolate in the top of a double boiler; bring the water to a boil. Reduce heat to low; cook until the chocolate melts, stirring constantly. Stir in the strawberry mixture. Add the vanilla; stir well.

3. Pour the chocolate mixture into an ungreased 9" square pan lined with plastic wrap. Cover and chill for at least 8 hours.

4. Cut the chocolate mixture into 64 squares with a hot knife. Working quickly, shape each square into a ball; roll in the chopped almonds. Store in the refrigerator. Serve at room temperature.

Yield: 64 truffles.

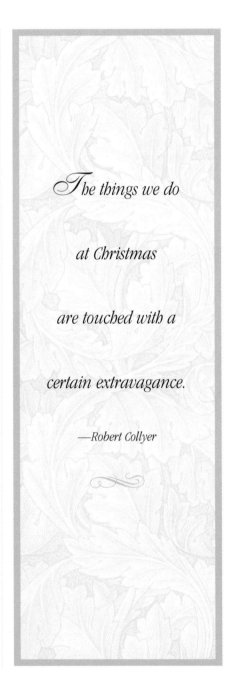

The things we do

at Christmas

are touched with a

certain extravagance.

—Robert Collyer

Shortbread looks especially appealing when given on a vintage plate. If your plate has a lacy edge, you may wish to weave wire-edged ribbon through the openings and tie the ends in a bow.

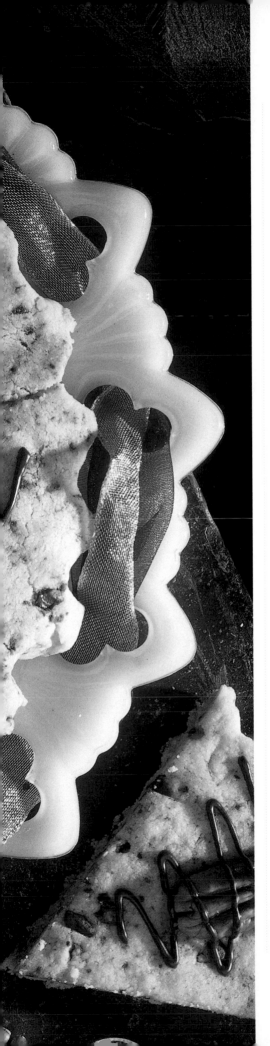

Chocolate-Pecan Shortbread

Score a circle of rich shortbread before baking so that it will break into wedges for serving. For a pretty finish, attach and decorate pecan halves using melted chocolate.

1   cup butter, softened
⅓   cup sugar
2   teaspoons vanilla extract
2½   cups all-purpose flour
½   cup finely chopped pecans, toasted
3   (1-ounce) squares semisweet
        chocolate, finely chopped
18   pecan halves
2   (1-ounce) squares semisweet
        chocolate, melted

1. Beat the butter in a large mixing bowl at medium speed of an electric mixer until creamy; gradually add the sugar, beating well. Add the vanilla extract; beat well. Add the flour, the chopped pecans, and the finely chopped chocolate, stirring just until blended.
2. Divide the dough into 3 equal portions. Place 1 portion of the dough on an ungreased cookie sheet; roll into a 6" circle. Flute the edge of the dough with the handle of a wooden spoon or with your fingertips. Score the dough into 6 triangles. Repeat the procedure with the remaining 2 portions of dough.
3. Bake at 325° for 30 minutes. Let cool on the cookie sheets for 5 minutes. Remove from the cookie sheets and let cool completely on wire racks. Carefully separate the disks into wedges.
4. Brush the bottoms of the pecan halves with the melted chocolate;

place 1 pecan half, chocolate side down, in the center of each wedge. Spoon the remaining melted chocolate into a small zip-top plastic bag; snip a tiny hole in 1 corner. Pipe the chocolate over the pecan halves.
    Yield: 18 shortbread wedges.

Coconut-Vanilla Fudge

Thickened with vanilla wafer crumbs and chunky pecans, Coconut-Vanilla Fudge is an inspiring recipe for the novice cook.

2   cups vanilla wafer crumbs
1   cup flaked coconut
1   cup chopped pecans
2   cups sugar
½   cup butter or margarine
1   (5-ounce) can evaporated milk

1. Combine the first 3 ingredients; set aside.
2. Combine the sugar, the butter, and the evaporated milk in a heavy 3-quart saucepan. Cook over medium heat until the mixture comes to a boil, stirring gently; boil 3 minutes, stirring gently.
3. Remove from the heat; stir in the crumb mixture. Immediately pour the mixture into a buttered 8"- or 9"-square pan (the mixture will be soft but will harden as it cools). Cool completely before cutting into squares.
    Yield: 2¼ pounds.

Caramel-Pecan Fudge

Here is a memory in the making: Caramelize the sugar in a cast-iron skillet just the way your grandmother did.

4   cups sugar, divided
¼   cup butter or margarine
1   (12-ounce) can evaporated milk
1   cup chopped pecans, toasted
2   teaspoons vanilla extract

1. Place 1 cup sugar in a cast-iron skillet; cook over medium heat, stirring constantly with a wooden spoon, until the sugar melts and turns golden brown.
2. Butter the sides of a heavy 3-quart saucepan. Combine the remaining 3 cups sugar, the butter, and the evaporated milk in the pan; cook over medium-low heat, stirring constantly, until the sugar dissolves. Gradually add the caramelized sugar to the butter mixture (the mixture will form lumps, becoming smooth again as it cooks).
3. Cook over medium heat, stirring constantly, until the mixture comes to a boil. Cover and cook 2 to 3 minutes to wash down the sugar crystals from the sides of the pan. Uncover and cook, without stirring, until the mixture reaches the soft ball stage or until a candy thermometer registers 236°.
4. Remove from the heat; add the pecans and the vanilla. Stir vigorously exactly 5 minutes. Quickly pour the mixture into a buttered 8"- or 9"-square pan. Cool completely before cutting into squares.

Yield: 2½ pounds.

Old-Fashioned Chocolate Fudge

Custom-make this confection to suit your recipient's taste, choosing between mild milk chocolate or semisweet morsels.

2   cups sugar
1   cup evaporated milk
2   tablespoons light corn syrup
½   (12-ounce) package milk chocolate or semisweet chocolate morsels (1 cup)
¾   cup chopped pecans (optional)
¼   cup butter or margarine
2   teaspoons vanilla extract

1. Butter the sides of a heavy 3-quart saucepan. Combine the first 3 ingredients in the pan; cook over medium-low heat, stirring constantly, until the sugar dissolves.
2. Cook the mixture over medium-low, without stirring, until it comes to a boil. Cover and cook 2 to 3 minutes to wash down the sugar crystals from the sides of the pan. Uncover and cook, without stirring, until the mixture reaches the soft ball stage or until a candy thermometer registers 236°, adjusting heat as needed to maintain the mixture at a rolling boil.
3. Remove from the heat; without stirring, add the chocolate and the remaining ingredients to the pan. Cool, without stirring, 20 minutes or until the thermometer reaches 140°.
4. Stir vigorously just until the mixture thickens and begins to lose its gloss, about 5 minutes. Quickly pour the mixture into a buttered 8" square pan. Cool completely before cutting into squares.

Yield: 1½ pounds.

Peanut Butter Fudge

This fudge is made according to the traditional method, which requires a sure sense of timing. Work quickly when you pour the warm fudge into the pan.

2½   cups sugar
¾   cup butter or margarine
1   (5-ounce) can evaporated milk
1   cup creamy or crunchy peanut butter
1   (7-ounce) jar marshmallow cream
1   teaspoon vanilla extract

1. Butter the sides of a heavy 3-quart saucepan. Combine the first 3 ingredients in the pan; cook over medium heat until the mixture comes to a boil, stirring gently. Cover and cook 2 to 3 minutes to wash down the sugar crystals from the sides of the pan. Uncover and cook, without stirring, 5 minutes.
2. Remove from the heat; add the peanut butter and the marshmallow cream, stirring until well blended. Add the vanilla; stir vigorously 2 minutes. Quickly pour the mixture into a buttered 13" x 9" x 2" pan, spreading evenly. Cool completely before cutting into squares.

Yield: 2½ pounds.

Three ways to please, clockwise from left: **Peanut Butter Fudge, Caramel-Pecan Fudge,** *and* **Old-Fashioned Chocolate Fudge.** *Present an assortment in an antique tin.*

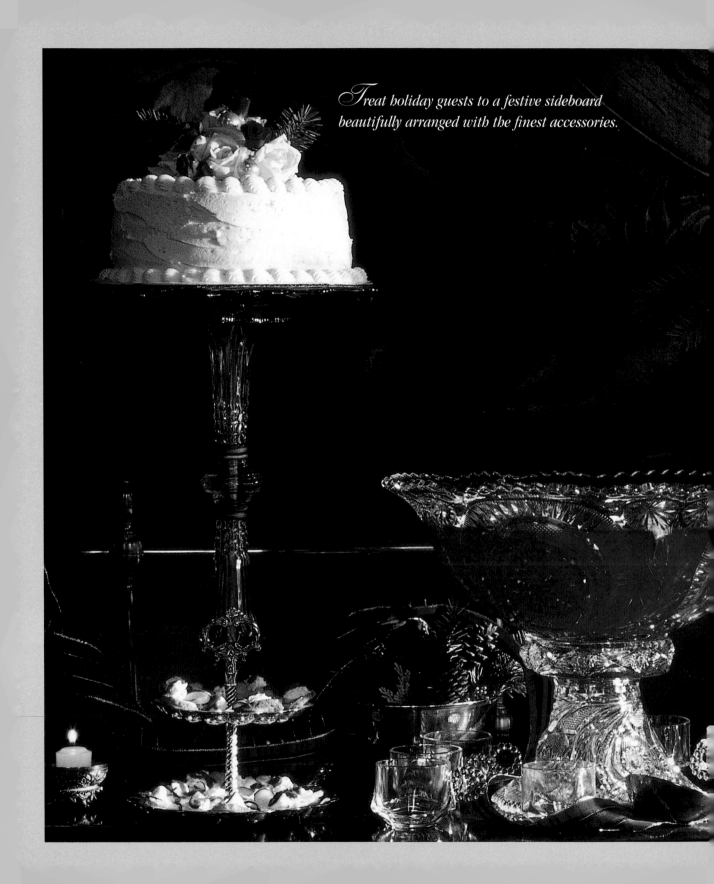

Treat holiday guests to a festive sideboard beautifully arranged with the finest accessories.

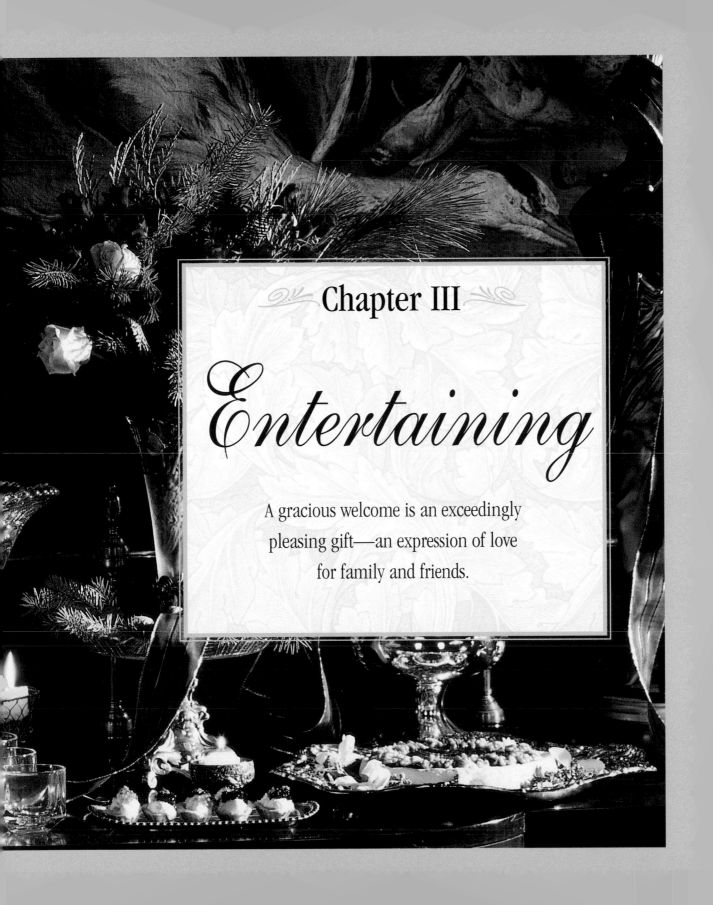

Chapter III

Entertaining

A gracious welcome is an exceedingly
pleasing gift—an expression of love
for family and friends.

Amaryllis blooms bring height to this sideboard display. A tumble of evergreens provides texture.

Bountiful Settings

*A handsomely appointed table and the thoughtful presentation of
a fine meal let every guest know this time is special.*

Because Christmas comes but once a year, it is fitting to celebrate with the finest traditions. One of the most welcome: a seated dinner at a table displaying your best linens, silver, china, and crystal. Orchestrated with your own personal style, it may well be one of the season's most memorable occasions.

As with most events, setting the stage is the first course of action. Whether Christmas dinner will be served at the big table in the dining room or at a smaller table pulled fireside, the view beyond the table is as important as the table setting. Allowing for a glimpse of a crackling fire or the lighted Christmas tree is always enjoyable. Decorate your sideboard for the season with an abundant arrangement of flowers and fruit in crystal and creamware.

Serve your guests at a formally set table or, for ease, offer the meal buffet style. On the sideboard, elegantly present the meal amid fresh greenery and decorations.

At the conclusion of the meal, suggest that guests move into the living room for coffee, liqueurs, and desserts. Good conversation will certainly follow.

Double napkins adorned with berries and a satin ribbon bow complement this place setting.

Christmas tree lights sparkle on a fireside table set for four. Gold-rimmed china, polished silver, and mirror-bright crystal glisten against a white linen cloth edged in lace.

Though it is snowing outside, guests will be warm at teatime while being served in the glow of the shimmering Christmas lights.

Stay for coffee. Drop by for tea. Join us for dessert. These may be the most sought-after invitations this Christmas season. Such occasions, at which light fare and a soothing beverage are offered, provide a recess from the hurry of shopping and decorating. As such, they present an ideal way to entertain small groups before or after a concert or a church service.

The menu is gratifyingly simple. With coffee or tea, offer both sweet and savory delicacies. At a dessert party, make sure the treats are of the most indulgent sort.

Plan to serve your guests in the parlor near the Christmas tree, in the sun-room, or in the library. Since a measure of serendipity is already in play, follow through with easygoing consideration of the details. Arrange the desserts on the sideboard with hot cider, eggnog, or holiday punch served in a crystal or silver punch bowl. Mix the patterns of your china cups and saucers. Brew a lovely pot of tea. And station the coffee urn so that guests can refill their cups at their leisure.

A splendid silver urn is a glamorous centerpiece; you need only a cluster of roses to complete the setting.

On the Side

Few pieces of furniture are as functional as a sideboard, also known as a huntboard. Tall serving tables that usually include some storage space, sideboards were widely produced in America during the eighteenth and early nineteenth centuries. Some of the oldest surviving pieces are simply designed, while more elaborate versions feature intricate inlays, fine brass hardware, and unusual combinations of side and front drawers.

Antique sideboards and modern reproductions can be pressed into service with great style during the Christmas season. Besides its original role as a service for buffets, the sideboard is also well suited for displaying still lifes of ornaments and greenery. For the most impact, vary the heights of items, using pedestals, vases, and candlesticks of varying statures. Center a large item like a punch bowl on the sideboard and roughly repeat the objects that flank it.

A jolly trio of Fathers Christmas perches amid a treasured collection of blue-and-white Spode plates and platters.

Essential Elements

China, crystal, and silver are the ingredients for an unforgettable table.

Special China

This season, display your loveliest china, setting the table to suit your fancy.

What a pleasure it is to bring out the treasured china pieces that you've collected over the years and set aside for special occasions.

Popular holiday china patterns feature holly and berries, ribbon bows, and Christmas colors.

Let the celebration also include the china you love and use year-round, even if the colors and patterns are not typically Christmassy. Festively combine your special china with your Christmas decorations, arranged in the china cabinet or on the sideboard. Charm guests with a table set with mismatched plates so that each individual place setting has its own special appeal.

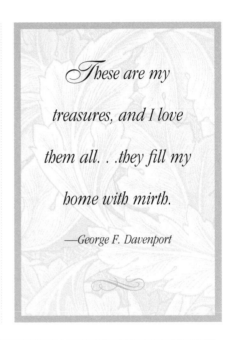

These are my treasures, and I love them all. . .they fill my home with mirth.

—*George F. Davenport*

The Teapot

Newly minted, antique, or reproduction teapots are popular collectibles. And collectors know well the history of the teapot. When tea and teaware first were imported from China to England in the seventeenth century, only the wealthy could afford them.

In the 1760s British potter Josiah Wedgwood perfected the process for making teapot creamware from a durable, light-colored earthenware. His lasting contribution made china affordable to the then-growing English upper middle class. Designs from the period still can be found, ranging from delicate to jauntily whimsical, from large to small enough for only one cup. Wedgwood's creamware remains popular, and several patterns are still in production.

Check the underside of a china teapot or other serving piece to determine its vintage: If it bears no mark, it was almost certainly made before 1891, the date from which the United States government began requiring imported china to indicate its country of origin. Pieces labeled with only the country's name were likely made between 1891 and 1914.

May you have the gladness of Christmas / Which is hope,

The spirit of Christmas / Which is peace,

The heart of Christmas / Which is love.

—Ada V. Hendricks

Toasting the Season

Fine crystal lends ceremony to every sip.

What drink to have with the holiday dinner? Serve what flatters your taste buds. You may select a white, red, or blush wine, perhaps a sparkling wine or champagne, followed by a dessert wine or port. Each has its own fine qualities, and each requires a glass shape that brings out its best.

Reds, blushes, and whites work equally well in an all-purpose wineglass whose bowl is slightly wider than the rim. Red wines are ideally served in a glass large enough to allow room for swirling, which releases the bouquet of the wine. Sparkling wines and champagnes are suited to the flute, whose tapered shape slows the release of the tiny bubbles. Small, tulip-shaped glasses are best for port, sherry, and Madeira wines, as well as for liqueurs. Brandy should be served in a snifter, a short-stemmed, bowl-shaped vessel designed to be held in the palm.

A lyrical gold border enhances the graceful bowls of these brandy snifters. Hold a glass in your palm so that the warmth of your hand will release the liquor's fragrance.

Champagne flutes—some gently curved like tulips, others long and slightly flared—preserve the effervescence of the merriest of drinks.

Toasted rounds peek from beneath the lid of a silver biscuit tin.

A Shining Silver Service

Silver is the perfect marriage of form and function.

There was a time when brides knew the excitement of receiving a set of silver flatware. If such a set has made its way to you, it likely is among your most prized possessions.

And if your set bears the monogram of its original owner, you will surely honor the legacy when your table is set with an array of flatware and serving pieces—not just at Christmas, but all the year through. That is because both sterling silver and its practical cousin silver plate look best when frequently used. The brightness of new silver softens to a beautiful patina that cannot come from polishing—it must be acquired over time.

A repoussé silver pepper shaker is paired with a silver salt cellar, a tiny footed bowl. The centerpiece of lilies is lovely on a repoussé tray, featuring a pattern of roses and daisies.

A tiered silver pastry stand, set on a silver tray, is both beautiful and useful.

Special Finds

Part of the fun of owning a set of antique silver is trying to identify each piece: tongs for sugar, asparagus, and ice; shakers for sugar, salt, and cinnamon; spoons for berries, melons, and soft-boiled eggs; and forks for pickles, potatoes, oysters, and olives. Details took on a particular importance during the Victorian age, and silversmiths were employed to design pieces for every imaginable culinary use.

Simple lines were less favored then than were the most elaborate forms. Period pieces often feature ornate decorations formed by gilding, in which gold is applied to the surface; by filigreeing, in which fine strands of wire are soldered on; or by embossing, also called repoussé, in which the silver is punched and stretched into a pattern.

An engraved menu card with a holiday motif announces the forthcoming feast. Folded tent-style, a handwritten place card indicates each guest's seat.

Miss Williamson

Black Truffle Soup

Endive and Orange Salad

Roast Partridge with Chanterelles
Celery Root Purée
Buttered Brussels Sprouts

Cranberry Ginger Tart

Beautiful Extras

Your loving attention to the details makes guests feel at home in your house.

Conversation Pieces

Plan a centerpiece that allows guests to comfortably see one another without craning. Low bowls of flowers or fruits are lovely. So are small arrangements and votives at each place setting. Ring hurricane lamps with greenery at the ends or at the center of the table to keep views unobstructed.

Hospitality is the art of making guests feel at ease. These gestures bring welcome grace to the table, be the setting grand or modest.

Menu Cards

Let beautifully scripted cards outline the meal to come. Use plain or bordered cards to match your holiday decorations and either handwrite or engrave the menu you have chosen so carefully. Set the cards in card holders at each place setting or lay them flat between two settings. If you are serving from a buffet, place a card at each end of the sideboard or the table. Or you may wish to letter a card to set beside each dish or platter on the buffet. Either way, your guests will appreciate knowing what you have prepared.

Place Cards

A handwritten place card at each setting will help guests seat themselves at the table. Arrange the places as you prefer or make a bow to convention. The protocol for seating guests relies on customs handed down from the Victorians because the traditional ways still make perfect sense: Seat the most honored guest at the host's right and seat the next most honored to the host's left. Or you may seat them at the center of the table.

To mark each place, set a flat card on the napkin in the center of the plate, in a silver or crystal place card holder, or against a tiny vase or crystal votive at each place. Or position a folded card tent-style on the table above the place setting, perhaps with a ribbon or a holly sprig decorating the card.

Sweet courtesy has

done its most

if you have made

each guest forget

that he himself

is not the host.

—*Thomas Bailey Aldrich*

No matter how gracefully the table is dressed, it must hold the most utilitarian of items: napkins, glasses, dishes, and trays. Let your imagination guide you to creative combinations.

Napkins

Cutwork, damask, linen, and cotton—each has a place at the holiday table and can be considered a decorative element. Slipcover lace napkins with festive squares of red-and-green tartan and then roll and tie them with black velvet ribbon. Fold crisp cotton or linen napkins into envelopes that hold party favors or pleat them into fans and place them in goblets or wineglasses. If you are using cutwork or monogrammed napkins, fold them so that the decorative stitching shows.

Napkin Rings

In the days when linens could not be laundered easily, an engraved or monogrammed ring kept each family member's napkin in place for the next meal. Today, the napkin ring is almost purely decorative, signifying that this is a special meal.

Collect antique napkin rings of silver, ceramic, or gold, or fashion your own from velvet or satin ribbon and greenery. Tie a small Christmas ornament around a napkin with a bit of golden cording or weave a ring of grapevine for a rustic look.

A touch of greenery and bows of red velvet ribbon elegantly decorate crisp white napkins.

Velvet ribbon napkin rings hold lacy white napkins wrapped in festive Christmas plaid.

Surrounded by evergreens and flowers, the gracious Christmas feast awaits friends and family.

Chapter IV
Christmas Dinner

The silver is polished, the table is set, and
the best part of Christmas is upon us:
A feast of memories to last the year through.

Christmas Dinner

Christmas appeals to all the senses, but perhaps to taste most of all. The holiday dinner must include the family's traditional recipes, but also may offer yet undiscovered pleasures. From our menu, choose new recipes you'll treasure for generations.

MENU

APPETIZERS: Choose one or two.
Wild Mushroom-Walnut Spread on Garlic Toasts
Cinnamon-Coffee Pecans   Cranberry-Glazed Brie

BEVERAGES: Choose one or two.
Spiced Coffee-Eggnog   Cranberry Champagne
Hot Buttered Wassail

SOUPS: Choose one.
Shrimp Bisque   Acorn Squash Soup

ENTRÉES: Choose one or two.
Roast Goose with Molasses Glaze and Apricot Stuffing
Cranberry Ham
Herb-Glazed Turkey with Wild Mushroom and Leek Stuffing

SIDE DISHES: Choose two to four.
Bourbon-Laced Sweet Potatoes
Corn Pudding with Crabcake Topping
Green Beans with Balsamic-Glazed Onions
Mapled Brussels Sprouts   Potato and Pear Tart
Black and Green Olives in Citrus-Mustard Vinaigrette
Cranberry-Walnut Relish   Corn Relish

BREADS: Choose one or two.
Thyme Biscuits with Red Currant Jelly
Orange-Rosemary Pinwheels   Gruyère Rolls

DESSERTS: Choose one or both.
Sour Cream Pound Cake with Dried Fruit Compote
Bread Pudding with Whiskey Sauce

Wild Mushroom-Walnut Spread on Garlic Toasts

You may want to serve these savory hors d'oeuvres with the main course for a delectable dinner accompaniment.

3   ounces dried wild mushrooms
1½   cups hot water
1   cup whipping cream
3   tablespoons Cognac
½   cup minced green onions
3   large cloves garlic, minced and divided
¼   cup olive oil
1   (3-ounce) package cream cheese, softened
¾   cup toasted walnuts, minced
1   cup chopped fresh parsley
3   tablespoons chopped fresh thyme
3   tablespoons chopped fresh chives
2   tablespoons chopped fresh tarragon
1½   teaspoons salt
¾   teaspoon freshly ground pepper
5   tablespoons butter or margarine, melted
1   French baguette, cut into ¼" slices

1. Rinse the mushrooms thoroughly with cold water; drain well. Combine the mushrooms and hot water in a medium bowl; let stand 2 hours. Drain well. Coarsely chop the mushrooms; set aside.
2. Combine the whipping cream and Cognac in a heavy saucepan. Bring almost to a boil; reduce heat and simmer, uncovered, 20 to 30 minutes or until reduced to ¾ cup, stirring occasionally.
3. Cook the green onions and 2 cloves minced garlic in hot oil in a large skillet over medium-high heat, stirring constantly, until tender. Add the mushrooms; cook 5 minutes, stirring constantly. Add the whipping cream mixture and cream cheese, stirring until the cream cheese melts. Remove from heat; stir in the walnuts and next 6 ingredients. Set aside.
4. Combine the melted butter and 1 clove minced garlic. Brush both sides of the bread slices with the garlic butter; place on an ungreased baking sheet. Bake at 350° for 6 to 8 minutes; turn and bake 5 additional minutes or until golden.
5. Spread 1 tablespoon of the mushroom mixture on each piece of toast.

Yield: about 40 appetizers.

Cinnamon-Coffee Pecans

This appetizer blends the delicious tastes of cinnamon, coffee, and coconut.

3   cups pecan halves
½   cup sugar
¼   cup water
1   tablespoon instant coffee granules
¾   teaspoon ground cinnamon
A pinch of salt
1   teaspoon coconut extract

1. Spread the pecan halves on an ungreased 15" x 10" x 1" jellyroll pan. Bake at 350° for 10 minutes, stirring after 5 minutes.
2. Combine the sugar and next 4 ingredients in a medium saucepan. Cook over medium heat, stirring frequently, until the sugar dissolves. Add the pecans and cook 3 minutes, stirring constantly. Remove from heat and stir in the coconut extract.
3. Spread the pecans on an ungreased jellyroll pan. Bake at 300° for 15 to 20 minutes, stirring every 5 minutes. Let cool completely; store in an airtight container.

Yield: 3 cups.

Cranberry-Glazed Brie

A tasty prelude to dinner begins with a round of Brie dressed in a red cranberry sauce.

1   (12-ounce) package fresh cranberries
¾   cup firmly packed brown sugar
⅓   cup currants
⅓   cup water
⅛   teaspoon dry mustard
⅛   teaspoon ground ginger
⅛   teaspoon ground cardamom
⅛   teaspoon ground allspice
⅛   teaspoon ground cloves
1   (35.2-ounce) round Brie
Garnish: fresh fruit

1. Combine the first 9 ingredients in a medium saucepan. Cook over medium heat, stirring constantly, 8 minutes or until the cranberry skins pop. Set aside and let cool.
2. Remove the rind from the top of the Brie, cutting to within ½" of the outside edges. Place the cheese on a baking sheet; spoon the cranberry mixture over the top of the Brie. Bake at 300° for 20 to 25 minutes or until the cheese is softened, but not melted.
3. Transfer the cheese to a serving platter; garnish with fresh fruit. Serve with assorted crackers.

Yield: 18 appetizer servings.

*S*piced **Coffee-Eggnog** *adds the flavor of coffee to a Christmas custom. And sparkling* **Cranberry Champagne** *(opposite) benefits from a touch of pineapple juice.*

Spiced Coffee-Eggnog

Served in your finest crystal, this frothy eggnog begins the celebration.

2   cups strong brewed coffee
1½ (3") sticks cinnamon
6   whole allspice
6   whole cloves
2   (32-ounce) cans eggnog, chilled
1   tablespoon vanilla extract
1   cup whipping cream, whipped
1   quart vanilla ice cream, softened
Ground nutmeg

1. Combine the first 4 ingredients in a saucepan. Bring to a boil; reduce heat and simmer, uncovered, for 15 minutes. Pour the coffee mixture through a wire-mesh strainer into a bowl; discard the spices. Chill.
2. Combine the coffee mixture, eggnog, and vanilla extract in a large bowl; fold in the whipped cream. Spoon the softened ice cream into a punch bowl. Pour the eggnog mixture over the ice cream and stir gently. Sprinkle the punch with ground nutmeg.

Yield: 11 cups.

Cranberry Champagne

Frozen cubes of pineapple juice and fresh cranberries keep this tart beverage cool. Freeze the flavored ice cubes for up to two weeks.

2   (48-ounce) bottles cranberry-
      raspberry drink, chilled
1   (12-ounce) can frozen pineapple
      juice concentrate, thawed
Cranberry Ice Cubes
2   (750-milliliter) bottles dry
      champagne

1. Combine the cranberry-raspberry drink and pineapple juice; stir well.
2. To serve, pour the mixture into a large punch bowl; stir well. Add the Cranberry Ice Cubes. Stir in the champagne just before serving.

Yield: 20 cups.

Cranberry Ice Cubes
2   cups pineapple juice, divided
½   cup sugar
1   (12-ounce) package fresh cranberries

1. Combine 1 cup pineapple juice and sugar in a medium saucepan. Bring to a boil; reduce heat and simmer until the sugar dissolves.
2. Add the cranberries. Bring to a boil over medium heat and cook 5 minutes or just until the cranberry skins begin to pop. Remove from heat and let cool.
3. Spoon the cranberry mixture evenly into about 2½ ice cube trays. Pour the remaining 1 cup pineapple juice evenly over the cranberry mixture. Freeze until firm.

Yield: 34 cubes.

Hot Buttered Wassail

The Anglo-Saxons gave us the word for wassail: "waes hael," which translates to "be in good health." Extend this warm greeting on Christmas, New Year's, and Twelfth Night.

2   quarts apple cider
2   cups ginger ale
2   cups orange juice
1   (3-ounce) package orange-
      pineapple-flavored gelatin
½   cup lemon juice
1   lemon, sliced and studded with
      whole cloves
2   small apples, halved lengthwise
3   (3") sticks cinnamon
½   cup butter, softened
¼   cup firmly packed brown sugar
¼   cup maple syrup

1. Combine the first 8 ingredients in a large Dutch oven; stir well. Bring the mixture to a boil. Reduce heat and simmer, covered, 30 minutes.
2. Beat the butter at medium-high speed of an electric mixer until creamy; gradually add the brown sugar and maple syrup, blending until creamy. Use the butter mixture immediately or cover and chill. Before using, let the butter mixture return to room temperature.
3. To serve, place 1 heaping tablespoon butter mixture into individual cups; fill with the hot wassail and stir well. Serve immediately.

Yield: 13 cups.

Shrimp Bisque

Homemade fish stock is the secret ingredient in this soup. Prepare it a day ahead to enhance the seasoning.

1   pound unpeeled medium-size fresh shrimp
3   tablespoons butter or margarine
3   tablespoons all-purpose flour
1   medium onion, chopped
2   stalks celery, chopped
2   cloves garlic, crushed
1   sweet red pepper, coarsely chopped
4   cups Fish Stock
1   (8-ounce) can tomato sauce
2 or 3 dashes of hot sauce
1   bay leaf
¼   teaspoon paprika
Garnish: fresh chives

1. Peel the shrimp and devein, if desired; set aside. Melt the butter in a Dutch oven over medium heat; add the flour, stirring until smooth. Cook, stirring constantly, 5 minutes or until golden.
2. Stir in the onion, celery, and garlic; cook about 3 minutes, stirring constantly. Stir in the sweet red pepper; cook 1 minute. Gradually add the stock and next 4 ingredients.
3. Bring to a boil, stirring occasionally. Reduce heat and simmer 5 minutes.
4. Add the shrimp; cook 5 minutes or until the shrimp turn pink. Remove and discard the bay leaf. Spoon into individual bowls; garnish with fresh chives.

Yield: 6½ cups.

Fish Stock

2   leeks
6 to 9 sprigs fresh parsley
1   large bay leaf
4   sprigs fresh basil
4   sprigs fresh rosemary
3   sprigs fresh thyme
2   (2" x ½") strips lemon rind
2   (2" x ½") strips orange rind
2   tablespoons butter or margarine
1   medium onion, sliced
½   carrot, sliced
2   stalks celery with leaves, coarsely chopped
3   pounds fish bones and shrimp shells
6   whole peppercorns
2   quarts water
1   cup dry white wine
½   teaspoon salt

1. Remove the roots, outer leaves, and green tops from the leeks, reserving 2 pieces of the tops. Split the white portions in half lengthwise and wash; set aside. Trim the reserved green pieces; place the parsley and next 6 ingredients on the top of 1 green piece; top with the other green piece of the leek and tie with string. Set the bouquet garni aside.
2. Melt the butter in a stockpot over medium heat. Add the leek, onion, carrot, and celery; cook, stirring constantly, until tender. Add the bouquet garni, bones and shells, and next 3 ingredients. Bring to a boil; cover, reduce heat, and simmer 30 minutes.
3. Line a wire-mesh strainer with a double layer of cheesecloth; place in a bowl. Pour the stock into the strainer; discard the solids. Stir in the salt; cool the stock slightly.
4. Cover and chill the stock. Remove and discard the solidified fat from the top of the stock. Cover the stock and chill up to 2 days, or freeze up to 1 month.

Yield: 1½ quarts.

Christmas has come; let

every man

Eat, drink, be merry all

he can.

. . . No matter what lies

in the bowls,

We'll make it rich with

our own souls.

—*William Henry Davies*

Acorn Squash Soup owes its rich color to a mixture of acorn squash and carrots.

Acorn Squash Soup

Dry sherry spikes this creamy soup. To keep flavors at their peak, warm the tureen and bowls before serving.

3   acorn squash
3   carrots, scraped and sliced
1   medium onion, sliced
3½ cups canned ready-to-serve chicken
      broth, divided
⅓   cup water, divided
2   tablespoons butter or margarine
1   tablespoon all-purpose flour
½   cup dry sherry
1   teaspoon salt
½ to 1 teaspoon black pepper
½   teaspoon ground nutmeg
⅛   teaspoon paprika
A pinch of ground allspice
A pinch of ground red pepper
1   cup half-and-half
Garnish: fresh thyme sprigs

1. Cut each squash in half lengthwise; remove the seeds. Place the halves, cut sides down, in a shallow pan; add hot water to the pan to a depth of 1". Bake, uncovered, at 350° for 55 minutes or until tender. Drain the squash halves on paper towels, cut sides down. Scoop out and reserve the pulp; discard the shells.

2. Cook the carrot and onion in boiling water to cover 12 to 15 minutes or until tender; drain. Combine half of the carrot mixture, half of the reserved squash pulp, ½ cup chicken broth, and half of the water in the container of an electric blender; cover and process until smooth. Repeat the procedure with the remaining carrot mixture, pulp, ½ cup chicken broth, and water; set aside.

3. Melt the butter in a Dutch oven over low heat; add the flour, stirring until smooth. Cook, stirring constantly, 1 minute. Gradually add the pureed mixture, remaining 2½ cups chicken broth, sherry, and next 6 ingredients; bring to a boil over medium heat. Cover, reduce heat, and simmer 1 hour, stirring occasionally. Stir in the half-and-half; cook just until thoroughly heated. (Do not boil.) Ladle the soup into individual bowls; garnish with fresh thyme sprigs.

Yield: 11½ cups.

*Present the **Roast Goose with Molasses Glaze** on a platter garnished with fresh fruit.*

Roast Goose with Molasses Glaze and Apricot Stuffing

Select a plump goose with clean, unblemished skin. Thaw a frozen goose in the refrigerator for two to three days.

MOLASSES GLAZE:
1   cup molasses
2   teaspoons bottled hot pepper sauce
1   teaspoon finely grated fresh
       gingerroot
1   teaspoon chopped garlic
½   teaspoon coarsely ground black
       pepper

ROAST GOOSE:
1 (10- to 12-pound) domestic goose
Salt to taste
Garnish: small apples and grapes
Apricot Stuffing

TO MAKE GLAZE:
In a bowl, combine the molasses, bottled hot pepper sauce, gingerroot, garlic, and pepper. Mix well and set aside.

TO PREPARE ROAST GOOSE:
1. Remove the giblets from the goose for later use. Rinse the goose in cold water, removing as much fat as possible from the body cavity. Pat the goose dry with paper towels.
2. Pierce the skin all over with a fork. Season the goose with salt inside and out. Arrange the goose, breast side up, on a rack in a roasting pan. Roast at 425° for 15 minutes.
3. Reduce the oven temperature to 350°. Continue roasting for 20 to 23 minutes per pound until a thermometer inserted between a leg and the thickest part of a thigh registers 180°. (Make sure the thermometer does not touch the bone.)
4. Drain off the fat from the pan. Brush the molasses glaze completely over the goose. Continue roasting 20 minutes, brushing with the molasses mixture after 10 minutes.
5. Remove the goose from the oven. Cover it with foil and let it stand for 15 minutes before carving. Arrange the goose on a serving platter. Garnish with apples and grapes. Carve the goose and serve with the Apricot Stuffing.

Apricot Stuffing

1   (8-ounce) onion, chopped
       (1¾ cups)
1   celery stalk, chopped (½ cup)
1   tablespoon vegetable oil
1   tablespoon minced garlic
½   tablespoon coarsley ground black
       pepper
1   tablespoon chopped fresh thyme
       or 1 teaspoon dried thyme
1   tablespoon chopped fresh parsley
1   tablespoon chopped fresh sage or
       ½ teaspoon dried rubbed sage
1   cup chopped dried apricots
2   cups coarsely crumbled day-old
       corn bread
Salt to taste
1   large egg
1½ cups rich chicken stock

1. While the goose is roasting, butter a deep 1½-quart baking dish. Set aside.
2. In a medium skillet, sauté the onion and celery in hot oil over medium-high heat for 4 to 5 minutes until soft.
3. Pour into a large bowl. Add the garlic and next 7 ingredients. Toss to mix. Set aside.
4. In a small bowl, whisk together the egg and stock. Pour over the stuffing. Mix well. (Mixture will appear soupy.) Pour into the prepared baking dish. Bake at 350° for 40 minutes until hot in the center.
    Yield: 6 to 8 servings.

Cranberry Ham

The holiday tastes of smoked ham and cranberry sauce make this recipe a new Christmas classic.

1   (5- to 7-pound) smoked fully
       cooked ham half
Whole cloves
1   (8-ounce) can jellied cranberry
       sauce
¼   cup firmly packed brown sugar
3   tablespoons cider vinegar
1   tablespoon commercial steak sauce
½   teaspoon dry mustard
¼   teaspoon ground allspice
¼   teaspoon ground cloves
2   tablespoons orange juice
1   bunch red grapes
Garnish: salad savoy

1. Remove and discard the skin from the ham. Score the fat on the ham in a diamond design and stud with the whole cloves. Place the ham, fat side up, on a rack in a shallow roasting pan. Insert a meat thermometer, making sure it does not touch the fat or the bone.
2. Combine the cranberry sauce and next 6 ingredients, stirring well. Baste the ham lightly with some of the cranberry mixture. Cover and bake at 325° for 1 hour. Uncover and baste the ham. Bake, uncovered, an additional hour or until the meat thermometer registers 140°, basting every 15 minutes.
3. Combine the orange juice and the remaining cranberry mixture in a skillet. Trim the grapes to make several small clusters. Add the grapes to the orange juice mixture; toss gently. Cook over low heat just until the grapes are glazed.

4. Transfer the ham to a serving platter. Add the glazed grapes. Garnish with salad savoy.
    Yield: 10 to 14 servings.

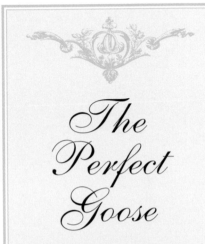

The Perfect Goose

The secret to a well-prepared goose, as well as other game birds, is adding moisture and robust flavor to the goose during cooking.

Basting the goose with a bold-tasting sauce will keep it moist and flavorful. Try sauces made with ruby, fruity wines or flavored vinegars.

Ideal accompaniments are braised chestnuts, Brussels sprouts, or intensely flavored dried or fresh fruits.

For a glorious main course, tartlets of **Corn Pudding with Crabcake Topping** *(page 106) surround a golden* **Herb-Glazed Turkey**.

Herb-Glazed Turkey with Wild Mushroom and Leek Stuffing

Roasted to perfection, a moist and flavorful turkey dressed with a wild mushroom stuffing will please your guests.

GLAZE:
1   cup honey, preferably Tupelo
¼   cup butter, melted
2   tablespoons minced fresh sage or 2 teaspoons crumbled dried sage leaves
1   tablespoon minced fresh basil or 1 teaspoon dried basil
1   tablespoon minced fresh parsley
Salt to taste
White pepper to taste
Black pepper to taste

ROAST TURKEY:
1   (16-pound) turkey, rinsed and patted dry
¼   cup olive oil
1   teaspoon salt
1   tablespoon minced fresh thyme or 1 teaspoon dried thyme
½   teaspoon white pepper
½   teaspoon black pepper
Wild Mushroom and Leek Stuffing

TO MAKE GLAZE:

In a bowl, combine all the ingredients for the glaze. Set aside.

TO PREPARE ROAST TURKEY:

1. Brush the turkey, inside and out, with the olive oil.

2. In a small bowl, combine the salt, thyme, and white and black peppers. Sprinkle the turkey with seasonings and transfer it to a rack in a roasting pan.

3. Roast the turkey at 325° for 2 hours. Brush the turkey with the glaze and continue roasting for 1½ to 2 hours more, basting frequently, until the juices run clear and a meat thermometer inserted in a thigh registers 180°.

4. Transfer the turkey to a serving platter and let it rest in a warm place for 20 minutes. Serve with stuffing.

Wild Mushroom and Leek Stuffing

8   cups coarsley crumbled day-old corn bread
7   cups fresh bread crumbs
2   cups milk
1   cup (½ pound) butter
4   cups finely chopped onion
3   cups finely chopped leek
1   cup finely chopped celery
5   cups sliced assorted mushrooms, such as white, shiitake, cremini, oyster
3   tablespoons minced garlic
7   large eggs, beaten lightly
¼   cup minced fresh basil or 4 teaspoons dried basil
3   tablespoons minced fresh thyme or 1 tablespoon dried thyme
3   tablespoons minced fresh parsley
¼   teaspoon salt or to taste
¼   teaspoon white pepper or to taste
¼   teaspoon freshly grated nutmeg
¼   teaspoon ground cloves
2   cups chicken stock or canned broth

1. In a large bowl, combine the corn bread and bread crumbs. Add the milk and let soak for 5 minutes.

2. In a large skillet, set over medium heat, melt half the butter, then add half each of onion, leek, and celery. Cook for 3 minutes, stirring occasionally. Add half the mushrooms and half the garlic, and then cook for 5 minutes, stirring occasionally. Transfer to the bowl with the corn bread. Repeat with the remaining butter, onion, leek, celery, mushrooms, and garlic.

3. Add the eggs and remaining ingredients; stir to combine.

4. Transfer to a large buttered baking dish and bake at 375° for 30 to 40 minutes or until the top is golden.

Yield: 12 to 15 servings.

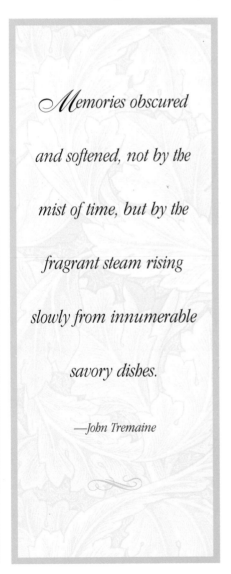

Memories obscured and softened, not by the mist of time, but by the fragrant steam rising slowly from innumerable savory dishes.

—*John Tremaine*

Bourbon-Laced Sweet Potatoes

For a formal dinner, pipe the potato mixture into the sweet potato shells using a large star tip.

6 medium-size sweet potatoes (about 4 pounds)
¼ cup butter or margarine, softened
½ cup firmly packed brown sugar
1 large egg
3 to 4 tablespoons bourbon
½ teaspoon ground cinnamon
⅓ cup flaked coconut
¼ cup chopped pecans
¼ cup firmly packed brown sugar
2 tablespoons butter or margarine

1. Wash the sweet potatoes; bake them at 375° for 1 hour or until done. Allow the potatoes to cool to the touch. Cut a lengthwise strip from the top of each potato and discard. Carefully remove the pulp, leaving ¼" thick shells intact.
2. Mash the potato pulp in a large bowl; add ¼ cup softened butter and stir until melted. Add ½ cup brown sugar and the next 3 ingredients; whip with a large wire whisk until very smooth. Spoon or pipe the mixture into the shells.
3. Combine the coconut, pecans, and ¼ cup brown sugar. Using a pastry blender, cut in 2 tablespoons butter until the mixture is crumbly. Sprinkle the coconut mixture over the potatoes. Place the stuffed potatoes on a baking sheet. Bake at 350° for 20 to 25 minutes or until thoroughly heated and lightly browned.
Yield: 6 servings.

Corn Pudding with Crabcake Topping

Whether baked in tartlet shells or in a casserole, this custardlike side dish holds a spicy crabmeat topping.

CORN PUDDING:
4 large eggs, beaten lightly
1 cup whipping cream
½ cup milk
½ teaspoon salt or to taste
½ teaspoon white pepper or to taste
¼ teaspoon hot sauce
8 ears corn, shucked and kernels removed or 8 cups corn kernels
¼ cup freshly grated Parmesan cheese
24 (4") prepared tartlet shells

CRABCAKE TOPPING:
½ pound crabmeat, picked over
1 large egg, beaten lightly
2 tablespoons bread crumbs
2 tablespoons snipped fresh chives
2 tablespoons grated carrot
2 tablespoons butter, melted
1 tablespoon lemon juice
1 tablespoon hot sauce
Salt and white pepper to taste

TO MAKE PUDDING:
1. In a bowl, combine the first 6 ingredients. Stir in the corn and cheese.
2. Transfer to the prepared tartlet shells or to a buttered, shallow baking dish to serve as a casserole.

TO MAKE TOPPING:
1. In a bowl, combine the crabmeat and remaining ingredients, stirring well. Set the mixture aside.
2. Bake the tartlets at 325° for 12 minutes, or bake the casserole at 325° for 25 minutes.

3. Top with the crabmeat and continue to bake the tartlets for 6 to 8 minutes more or the casserole for 10 to 12 minutes more or until the topping is golden.
Yield: 12 servings
(2 tartlets per person).

When Christmas tide

comes in like a bride,

With holly and ivy clad,

Twelve Days in the year

much mirth and good cheer

In every household

is had...

—L. Durfey Cinnamon

About Vinegars

For centuries, vinegar has been used for everything from beverages to antiseptics to hair rinses and softeners. By the seventeenth century, Europeans were seasoning vinegar with pepper, mustard, and garlic. A variety of vinegars will refine your favorite dishes:

• The exceptional taste of balsamic vinegar makes it ideal alone as a dressing for salad, fruit, or vegetables.

• Herb vinegars are perfect for adding flavor to foods. Sprinkle these vinegars over cooked broccoli, cauliflower, or vegetable soups. Fruit salads benefit from a touch of mint vinegar.

• Commercial hot pepper vinegar is made by steeping hot green chili peppers in vinegar, thus extracting their fiery flavor. A few drops will spice up soups and sauces.

• Blueberry-, raspberry-, or strawberry-flavored vinegar will enhance a vinaigrette dressing with its distinctive taste.

• Store all vinegars in a cool, dry place for up to six months.

Green Beans with Balsamic-Glazed Onions

Balsamic vinegar is a sweet Italian vinegar refined after years of aging.

6   tablespoons honey
¼   cup balsamic vinegar
¼   cup olive oil
½   teaspoon salt
½   teaspoon freshly ground pepper
1   (16-ounce) package frozen pearl onions, thawed and drained
1½   pounds fresh green beans

1. Combine the first 5 ingredients and divide in half. Combine half of the honey mixture and onions, tossing to coat. Spread the onion mixture in a lightly greased 15" x 10" x 1" jellyroll pan. Bake at 400° for 20 minutes or until the onions are tender and glazed, stirring occasionally.
2. Wash the beans; trim the ends and remove the strings. Cut the beans in half crosswise. Cook the beans in boiling salted water to cover 10 minutes or until tender; drain.
3. In a large bowl, combine the remaining half of the honey mixture, onions, and beans, tossing gently to coat. Serve immediately.
   Yield: 6 servings.

Mapled Brussels Sprouts

Honey mustard, horseradish, and hot maple syrup make a superb sauce for Brussels sprouts.

¼ cup unsalted butter
¼ cup pure maple syrup
2 tablespoons honey mustard
½ teaspoon cream-style prepared horseradish
Freshly ground pepper
2 pounds (8 cups) fresh Brussels sprouts

1. In a small saucepan, melt the butter over medium-low heat. Add the syrup, mustard, horseradish, and pepper. Whisk until smooth. Cook for 5 minutes, stirring occasionally. Remove from heat. Set aside.
2. Halve any large Brussels sprouts. Steam the sprouts for 12 to 15 minutes or until tender but still firm.
3. To serve, pour the hot maple sauce over the hot Brussels sprouts in a serving bowl. Toss gently to mix.
Yield: 8 servings.

Potato and Pear Tart

Bathed in a rich cream sauce, the flavors of pears and potatoes create this savory side dish.

TART PASTRY:
1¾ cups all-purpose flour
1 teaspoon salt
½ cup unsalted butter, softened
¼ cup ice water
Dried beans (to weight pastry)

SAUCE:
½ cup chopped leek
2 tablespoons dry white wine
2 cups whipping cream
¼ cup grated Romano cheese
Salt and pepper to taste

FILLING:
10 (2-ounce) small new potatoes, sliced ⅛" thick
3 (8-ounce) Anjou pears

TO MAKE PASTRY:
1. Butter a 10" tart pan. Set aside.
2. In a medium bowl, combine the flour and 1 teaspoon salt. With a pastry blender or 2 knives, cut in the butter until the mixture resembles coarse meal.
3. Gradually sprinkle the ice water over the dough, tossing with a fork until moist. Shape the dough into a ball. Form into a disk shape.
4. Wrap the dough in plastic wrap and refrigerate for at least 1 hour.
5. On a lightly floured surface, roll out the dough. Fit into the buttered tart pan, crimping the edge high at the top of the pan. Prick the pastry all over with the tines of a fork. Line the pastry with foil. Fill with the beans. Place the tart pan on a baking sheet.

6. Bake at 375° for 15 minutes. Remove the foil and beans. Bake the pastry for 10 minutes until lightly browned. Cool on a wire rack.

TO MAKE SAUCE:
1. In a heavy large pot, combine the leek, wine, and cream. Bring to a boil. Reduce heat and boil gently until reduced to 1½ cups, stirring often. (Watch carefully—the cream may boil high in the pot.)
2. Stir the cheese and salt and pepper into the sauce. Pour into a bowl. Press the plastic wrap directly on the surface of the sauce. Refrigerate until cold.

TO MAKE FILLING:
1. Reduce oven temperature to 350°. Line the cooled pastry shell with ⅓ of the potato slices in an overlapping layer. Spoon ¼ of the sauce over the potatoes, spreading evenly. Repeat with 2 more layers of the potatoes and sauce.
2. Peel, halve, and core the pears. Cut the pear halves crosswise in ¼" slices, keeping the slices intact. Angle the pear halves spoke-fashion over the potato filling, fanning out the slices slightly. Spoon the remaining sauce over the pears, coating completely. Place the tart pan on a baking sheet.
3. Bake at 350° for 1 hour until the potatoes in the center are tender. Cool on a wire rack for 20 minutes before serving in wedges.
Yield: 8 servings.

Anjou pears, a popular winter fruit, join new potatoes in a savory **Potato and Pear Tart**.

Relish platter stars:
Cranberry-Walnut Relish,
Black and Green Olives in Citrus-
Mustard Vinaigrette, *and* **Corn Relish.**

Black and Green Olives in Citrus-Mustard Vinaigrette

Seek quality olives for this relish. Use freshly squeezed juices for maximum results.

3   tablespoons cider vinegar
1   tablespoon orange juice
½   tablespoon lemon juice
¾   teaspoon lime juice
1   tablespoon Pommery (stone-ground) mustard
½   tablespoon Dijon mustard
½   cup vegetable oil
½   cup olive oil
⅛   teaspoon salt
⅛   teaspoon freshly ground pepper
1   (16-ounce) can black olives (preferably Kalamata), drained
1   (16-ounce) jar green olives (preferably Picholine), drained

1. In a deep medium bowl, combine the first 6 ingredients. Mix well.
2. Gradually whisk in the oils, salt, and pepper until blended. Add the olives, tossing to coat.
3. Cover and marinate the olives in the refrigerator overnight. Serve at room temperature. Remove the olives with a slotted spoon to serve.
    Yield: 3 cups.

Cranberry-Walnut Relish

Offer this spirited relish as a chutney with the main course. Spread leftovers on breakfast toast.

¼   cup brandy
1   teaspoon grated orange zest
¼   cup orange juice
¼   cup rice vinegar
¼   cup minced red onion
¼   teaspoon mustard seed
⅛   teaspoon salt
⅛   teaspoon freshly cracked pepper
1   cup sugar
1   (12-ounce) bag or 3 cups fresh cranberries
¾   cup toasted, chopped black walnuts

1. In a medium saucepan, combine the brandy, orange zest, orange juice, vinegar, onion, mustard seed, salt, and pepper. Bring to a boil over medium-high heat. Boil until the liquid is reduced to ¼ cup.
2. Reduce to medium heat. Stir in the sugar and cranberries. Cook, stirring until the sugar dissolves. Continue cooking for 9 minutes, stirring often, until most of the cranberries have popped.
3. Remove from heat. Stir in the walnuts. Cool. Pour into a serving dish. Cover. Refrigerate until serving time.
    Yield: 2½ cups.

Corn Relish

Marinate corn in a zesty blend of jalapeño, cilantro, and raspberry vinegar.

1   (16-ounce) package frozen whole-kernel corn
¼   cup minced onion
¼   cup chopped red pepper
1   teaspoon chopped garlic
½   teaspoon chopped jalapeño pepper
½   cup sugar
1   cup chicken stock
1   cup cider vinegar
1   tablespoon chopped fresh chives
1   teaspoon chopped fresh cilantro
½   teaspoon salt
½   teaspoon freshly cracked pepper
1   tablespoon raspberry vinegar

1. In a large saucepan, combine the first 8 ingredients. Bring to a boil, stirring until the sugar dissolves. Reduce heat. Simmer, uncovered, for 20 minutes until the corn is tender.
2. Remove from heat. Cool to room temperature, stirring occasionally.
3. Drain. Stir in the chives, cilantro, salt, and pepper. Mix well. Stir in the raspberry vinegar. Spoon into a serving dish.
4. Cover and refrigerate until serving time.
    Yield: 2½ cups.

Thyme Biscuits with Red Currant Jelly

The cardinal rule for making tender, flaky biscuits is this: Re-roll scraps only once.

2   cups all-purpose flour
2   teaspoons baking powder
½   teaspoon salt
2   tablespoons freshly chopped thyme or 2 teaspoons dried thyme
3   tablespoons unsalted butter
¾   cup milk
2   tablespoons whipping cream
2   tablespoons unsalted butter, melted
2   teaspoons red currant jelly
Garnish: fresh thyme sprigs

TO MAKE DOUGH:

1. Butter a baking sheet. In a large bowl, mix the flour, baking powder, salt, and thyme. Cut in 3 tablespoons butter until the mixture resembles coarse meal.
2. Combine the milk and cream. Gradually stir into the flour mixture with a fork until a soft dough forms. (The dough will be moist.)
3. Turn the dough out onto a well-floured surface. Knead gently with floured fingertips for 10 strokes.
4. Roll out the dough to a 12" diameter ¼" thick circle. Cut out the biscuits using a 2" heart cutter. Re-roll any scraps once.

TO ASSEMBLE:

1. Brush the hearts with the melted butter. Spoon ⅛ teaspoon jelly in the center of half the hearts. Moisten the edges with water, then top with the remaining hearts, buttered sides down. Gently press around the edges to seal.
2. Arrange the biscuits 1" apart on the baking sheet. Stick a wooden pick at an angle from the top through the bottom of each biscuit to prevent the top biscuit from sliding off during baking.
3. Bake at 450° for 12 to 15 minutes until golden. Remove the wooden picks and tuck in a small thyme sprig for garnish in place of the wooden pick.
Yield: 16 biscuits.

Orange-Rosemary Pinwheels

Substitute rosemary in the Thyme Biscuit dough recipe, then roll and bake.

Dough for Thyme Biscuits (left)
2   tablespoons unsalted butter, melted
¼   cup sugar
2   tablespoons grated orange zest

1. Generously butter and sugar a pan with 30 (1¾" diameter) miniature muffin cups.
2. Use the first 7 ingredients and follow steps 1, 2, and 3 in the recipe for Thyme Biscuit dough, substituting rosemary for the thyme. Roll out the dough onto a floured 8" x 15" rectangular surface. Cut the dough in half lengthwise to form 2 (4" x 15") rectangles.
3. Gently brush the melted butter over the dough. Sprinkle with the sugar and orange zest.
4. Roll up each piece of the dough jellyroll style, starting with the long side. Cut into 1" slices. Arrange each slice flat in a muffin cup. Set the pan on a baking sheet.
5. Bake at 450° for 12 to 15 minutes until golden.
Yield: 30 muffins.

Gruyère Rolls

If you prefer a milder cheese, switch Swiss for Gruyère. Either way, these rolls are a tasty treat.

3   cups all-purpose flour, divided
1   package rapid-rise yeast
1   cup (4 ounces) shredded Gruyère cheese
¼   teaspoon sugar
1   teaspoon salt
1¼   cups warm water (120° to 130°)

1. Combine 2¾ cups flour, yeast, and next 3 ingredients in a bowl. Gradually add the warm water to the mixture, beating at high speed of an electric mixer. Beat 2 additional minutes at medium speed. Gradually stir in enough of the remaining flour to make a soft dough.
2. Turn the dough out onto a floured surface and knead until smooth and elastic (about 10 minutes). Place in a well-greased bowl. Cover and let rise in a warm place (85°), free from drafts, 1 hour or until doubled in bulk.
3. Punch the dough down; turn out onto a lightly floured surface and knead lightly 4 or 5 times. Divide the dough in half. Shape each portion of the dough into 8 balls. Roll each ball in the flour; shape each portion into an oval.
4. Place the rolls 2" apart on a greased baking sheet. Cover and let rise in a warm place, free from drafts, 30 minutes or until doubled in bulk. Place the rolls in the oven; spray the rolls with water. Bake at 425° for 5 minutes, spraying after 3 minutes. Reduce heat to 350°; continue to bake, without spraying, 13 additional minutes or until golden. Remove from the baking sheet; let cool on a wire rack.
Yield: 16 rolls.

Baked from the same biscuit recipe, **Thyme Biscuits with Red Currant Jelly** *and* **Orange-Rosemary Pinwheels** *capture the essence of herbs.*

Moist **Sour Cream Pound Cake** *served with* **Dried Fruit Compote** *is the dinner's worthy finale.*

Sour Cream Pound Cake

Dress the sugared cake with a mound of fresh berries and a circlet of mint.

1½ cups (¾ pound) butter, softened
1⅔ cups sugar
½ teaspoon grated orange zest
¼ teaspoon ground cinnamon
9 large eggs
1 cup sour cream
2½ cups all-purpose flour
2 teaspoons baking powder
Garnish: sifted confectioners' sugar
and Dried Fruit Compote

1. Butter and flour a Bundt pan.
2. In a bowl with a mixer, beat the butter and the sugar. Beat in the zest and cinnamon.
3. In another bowl, beat the eggs until frothy. Add to the butter mixture in 4 additions, beating well after each addition.
4. Stir in the sour cream.
5. In a bowl, sift the flour and baking powder. Repeat sifting.
6. Add the flour mixture to the butter mixture in 2 additions, stirring just enough to combine after each addition.

7. Transfer the batter to the Bundt pan, smoothing the top, and bake at 300° for 1¼ to 1½ hours or until a wooden pick inserted in the center comes out clean.
8. Let cool in the pan 10 to 15 minutes; then invert onto a wire rack to cool completely. Sprinkle with confectioners' sugar and serve with Dried Fruit Compote.

Yield: 10 to 12 servings.

Dried Fruit Compote

A hint of fresh mint perks up dried cranberries, cherries, black currants, and raisins for a delightful pound cake sauce.

½ cup sugar
½ cup water
¼ cup maple syrup
1 (3") stick cinnamon
¼ cup dried cranberries
¼ cup dried cherries
¼ cup dried black currants
¼ cup golden raisins
1 teaspoon minced fresh mint or
to taste

1. In a saucepan, combine the first 4 ingredients. Bring to a boil, stirring well. Add the dried fruits and simmer 5 minutes.
2. Let cool to room temperature. Remove the cinnamon stick and stir in the mint.
3. Chill, covered, before serving, if desired.

Yield: 1¼ cups.

Pound Cake Points

Pound cake's name suggests its origins: a pound each of butter, sugar, flour, and eggs.

• Use the best ingredients for the best results: real butter, not margarine; real sour cream; Grade A large eggs; and real vanilla extract, not imitation. Substituting "light" versions of these ingredients will not lead to a lighter cake—in fact, they will have just the opposite effect.

• Whether beating by hand or with an electric mixer, do not overmix the batter, for it will adversely affect the texture.

• For the best finish, use a pastry brush to butter every crevice of the pan, especially if using a Bundt pan. Then coat the buttered pan with flour, and gently tap the inverted pan over the sink to shake out excess flour.

• Oven temperatures vary, so use the recipe's suggested baking time as a guide. To be sure your cake is done, insert a wooden pick into the center. If it comes out clean, the cake is ready to come out of the oven. If not, bake the cake for a few minutes more, and test again.

• Let the cake rest in the pan for 10 to 15 minutes, allowing it to shrink from the sides. Place a wire rack over the pan and invert to remove the cake, and then let it completely cool on the wire rack, where heat and moisture can escape evenly from all sides.

Bread Pudding with Whiskey Sauce

Stale bread meets its salvation when it is baked with raisins and vanilla in an egg-rich custard.

BREAD PUDDING:
1   (1-pound) loaf French bread or sliced white bread
1   quart milk
3   large eggs, beaten lightly
1½ cups sugar
1   cup raisins
2   tablespoons vanilla extract
3   tablespoons butter or margarine, melted

WHISKEY SAUCE:
½   cup butter
1   cup sugar
½   cup half-and-half
2   tablespoons whiskey

TO MAKE PUDDING:
1. Break the bread into pieces and put in a bowl. Add the milk and let soak 10 minutes; hand crush until blended. Add the eggs and next 3 ingredients.
2. Pour the butter into a greased 13" x 9" x 2" pan. Spoon the bread mixture into the pan; bake at 325° for 1 hour to 1 hour and 15 minutes or until the pudding is very firm.

TO MAKE WHISKEY SAUCE:
1. In a saucepan, combine the butter, sugar, and half-and-half. Cook over medium heat until the sugar dissolves.
2. Bring to a boil; reduce heat and simmer 5 minutes. Remove from heat. Let cool and add the whiskey. To serve, spoon the Whiskey Sauce over each serving.
   Yield: 12 to 15 servings.

Ruby raspberries and green sprigs of mint imbue this **Christmas Trifle** *(page 125) with the colors of Christmas.*

Chapter V

Holiday Sweets

A tempting trifle, a perfect cookie,
a quintessential Christmas pudding—
each an inspired gift in itself.

$\mathcal{L}$et Christmas be a journey paved with small celebrations. Bake sweet breads for a houseguest's breakfast tray, relax with cookies and tea when the shopping is done, and welcome neighbors with an array of desserts. Bring the journey to the happiest of endings with a glorious dessert after the grand family dinner.

Miniature Mince Pies

These tasteful treasures may preserve the peace over whose slice is biggest.

3 large eggs
4 cups all-purpose flour
2⅓ cups confectioners' sugar
1 cup unsalted butter
¾ cup Homemade Mincemeat
Garnish: confectioners' sugar

TO MAKE PASTRY:

1. In a small bowl, whisk the eggs. Set aside.
2. In a large bowl, combine the flour and 2⅓ cups confectioners' sugar. Mix well. With a pastry blender or 2 knives, cut in the butter until the mixture resembles coarse crumbs. Gradually add the eggs, tossing with a fork to moisten.
3. Knead the mixture gently in a bowl to form a soft dough. Divide the dough into quarters. Form each portion into a disk shape. Wrap and refrigerate 40 minutes.

TO ASSEMBLE:

1. On a well-floured surface, roll out ¼ of the dough to ⅛" thick. Cut into 6 (2½") rounds and 6 (2") rounds.
2. Fit the 2½" pastry rounds into 2" tart pans, patty tins, or individual brioche molds. Spoon ½ tablespoon mincemeat in the center of each tart.
3. Dampen the edges of the pastry. Top with the 2" pastry rounds. Press down around the edges to seal. Cut a tiny hole in the center top of each tart for steam to escape. Repeat with the remaining dough and mincemeat. Arrange the tart pans on baking sheets.
4. Bake at 400° for 12 to 15 minutes until lightly browned. Dust with the confectioners' sugar while warm. Remove from the pans. Serve warm.
Yield: 24 servings.

TO MAKE LARGE MINCE PIES:

1. Roll out ¼ of the pastry dough onto a well-floured surface. Fit into a 9" pieplate. Fill with 4 cups mincemeat. If desired, dot with 2 tablespoons butter. Roll out another ¼ of the dough. Place over the filling. Trim and flute the edge. Cut slits for steam to escape.
2. Place the pie on a baking sheet. Bake at 375° for 45 to 50 minutes until browned and the juices are bubbling. Cool on a wire rack. Repeat with the remaining pastry dough and mincemeat.
Yield: 2 pies.

Homemade Mincemeat

1⅓ cups dark raisins (8 ounces)
1⅓ cups golden raisins (8 ounces)
⅔ cup chopped candied peel (4 ounces)
1 pound baking apples, peeled, cored, and chopped (2½ cups)
3 cups currants (1 pound)
2¼ cups firmly packed brown sugar (1 pound)
1 teaspoon pumpkin pie spice
½ teaspoon ground ginger
¼ teaspoon ground nutmeg
Grated zest and juice of 2 lemons
⅔ cup brandy or rum

1. Chop the dark and golden raisins and the candied peel. Turn into a large bowl. Add the apple, currants, brown sugar, pumpkin pie spice, ginger, nutmeg, and lemon zest and juice. Mix well.
2. Cover and let stand overnight.
3. Stir in the brandy. Pack into sterilized jars. Cover and refrigerate up to 6 weeks. Stir well before using for Miniature Mince Pies.
Yield: 8 cups.

Treat holiday guests to fluffy **Scones** *(page 121) topped with strawberry jam and whipped cream and* **Miniature Mince Pies** *filled with chopped raisins, apples, and currants.*

Dust bite-sized **Pear and Hazelnut Bread** *with confectioners' sugar and garnish with strips of candied lemon peel.*

Pear and Hazelnut Bread

This fruit bread can be cut into dainty squares for tea. If you have leftover Pear Sauce, serve it with roast pork.

½   cup unsalted butter, softened
¾   cup firmly packed brown sugar
½   cup sugar
2   large eggs
1   cup Pear Sauce (room
      temperature)
2   cups all-purpose flour
1   teaspoon baking powder
½   teaspoon baking soda
½   teaspoon ground ginger
¼   teaspoon salt
Grated zest of 1 orange
¼   cup finely chopped crystallized
      ginger
½   cup finely chopped hazelnuts
Garnish: confectioners' sugar,
      crystallized ginger strips,
      and candied lemon peel

1. Butter and flour a 9" x 5" x 3" loaf pan. Line the bottom of the pan with waxed paper. Butter and flour the waxed paper.
2. In a small mixer bowl, beat the butter, brown sugar, and sugar at medium speed of an electric mixer until light and fluffy. Add the eggs and beat well. Beat in the Pear Sauce at low speed.
3. Sift together the flour, baking powder, baking soda, ground ginger, and salt. Gradually stir into the batter.
4. Add the orange zest, chopped crystallized ginger, and hazelnuts. Mix well. Spread evenly in the pan.
5. Bake at 350° for 60 to 65 minutes or until a wooden pick inserted in the center comes out clean.
6. Cool in the pan on a wire rack 10 minutes. Remove from the pan and cool on the rack.
7. Dust with the confectioners' sugar. Cut into squares or slices to serve. Garnish with crystallized ginger strips and candied lemon peel.

Yield: one 9" loaf.

Pear Sauce

5   (8-ounce) firm pears, peeled,
      quartered, and cored
1   lemon, peeled, quartered, and seeded
¼ to ½ cup sugar

1. In a food processor, chop the pears and lemon with on/off pulses in several batches (about 4 cups chopped fruit).
2. In a large saucepan, combine the fruit and sugar.
3. Bring to a boil. Reduce heat. Boil gently, stirring occasionally, about 30 minutes until the mixture reaches the consistency of applesauce.
4. Puree in a blender or processor, if desired.

Yield: 3⅓ cups.

Scones

Reward early risers with warm scones spread with strawberry jam and mounded with whipped cream.

6   tablespoons unsalted butter
3⅔   cups all-purpose flour
½   cup superfine sugar
2   teaspoons baking powder
3   tablespoons golden raisins (optional)
1 to 1¼ cups milk
Garnish: whipped cream and strawberry jam

1. In a large bowl with a pastry blender or 2 knives, cut the butter into the flour until the mixture resembles coarse crumbs. Add the sugar, baking powder, and raisins. Mix well.
2. Gradually add the milk, tossing gently with a fork until a soft dough forms. Turn out onto a floured surface. Knead gently with fingertips several strokes to form a smooth dough.
3. Roll out the dough 1½" thick. Cut out the scones with a deep 2" biscuit cutter. Arrange 2" apart on a non-stick baking sheet. Brush the tops lightly with additional milk.
4. Bake at 400° for 20 minutes until golden. Remove from the pan. Cool on a wire rack. Serve with whipped cream and strawberry jam.

Yield: 7 or 8 scones.

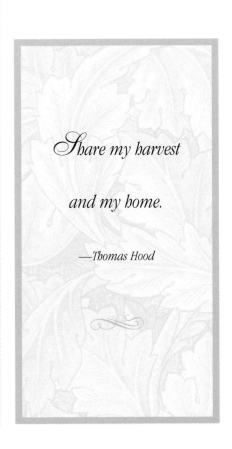

Share my harvest

and my home.

—*Thomas Hood*

Gocoa-Mint Cookies, **Chocolate-Hazelnut Sticks**, *and* **Raspberry-Filled Cookies** *(clockwise) are sweet surprises for Christmas get-togethers.*

Our hearts they hold all Christmas dear,
And earth seems sweet and heaven seems near.

—Marjorie L.C. Pickthall

Cocoa-Mint Cookies

A drizzle of pale green frosting on these cookies hints of the mint filling.

COOKIES:
1   cup butter or margarine, softened
⅔   cup sugar
1⅔ cups all-purpose flour
¼   cup cocoa
½   teaspoon vanilla extract
½   teaspoon chocolate menthe or
      mint flavoring
1   cup finely chopped pecans
3   dozen crème de menthe wafer
      thins, unwrapped (about
      6 ounces)

FROSTING:
1   cup sifted confectioners' sugar
1½ tablespoons milk
A few drops of green liquid food coloring

TO MAKE COOKIES:
1. Beat the butter at medium speed of an electric mixer until creamy; gradually add ⅔ cup sugar, beating well. Add the flour and cocoa, mixing well. Stir in the flavorings and pecans. Cover and chill 2 hours or until firm.
2. Shape the dough into 36 balls. Shape each ball into an oval around each crème de menthe wafer. Place on ungreased cookie sheets and chill 30 minutes.
3. Bake at 375° for 12 minutes. Cool slightly on the cookie sheets; remove the cookies to wire racks to cool completely.

TO MAKE FROSTING:
Combine the confectioners' sugar and milk, stirring until smooth; color with the green food coloring. Place in a heavy-duty, zip-top plastic bag.

Using scissors, snip a tiny hole in a bottom corner of the bag; drizzle the frosting over the cookies.

Yield: 3 dozen.

Chocolate-Hazelnut Sticks

You may substitute almonds, but the distinctive flavor of hazelnuts makes them worth the hunt.

⅔ cup whole hazelnuts or almonds
½ cup butter, softened
⅓ cup sugar
1 large egg
1½ teaspoons vanilla extract
⅛ teaspoon salt
½ teaspoon ground cinnamon
1¼ cups all-purpose flour
1 (6-ounce) package semisweet
    chocolate morsels
1 tablespoon shortening

1. Place the hazelnuts on a baking sheet and bake at 325° for 20 minutes, stirring occasionally. Cool 5 minutes; rub between your hands to loosen the skins. Discard the skins. Position the knife blade in a food processor bowl; add the hazelnuts and process until coarsely chopped. Set aside 3 tablespoons nuts for garnish and finely grind the remaining nuts. Increase the oven temperature to 350°.
2. Beat the butter at medium speed of an electric mixer until creamy; gradually add sugar, beating well. Add the egg, vanilla extract, salt, and cinnamon, beating until blended.
3. Add the flour, beating until smooth. Fold in the finely ground hazelnuts.

4. Use a cookie gun fitted with a star-shaped disc to shape the dough into decorative 2½" sticks, following the manufacturer's directions. Place the sticks on lightly greased cookie sheets.
5. Bake at 350° for 9 to 11 minutes or until lightly browned. Cool slightly on the cookie sheets; remove to wire racks to cool completely.
6. In the top of a double boiler, combine the chocolate morsels and shortening; bring the water to a boil. Reduce heat to low and cook until the chocolate melts. Dip one end of each cookie in the melted chocolate and sprinkle with the reserved nuts. Place on waxed paper to cool.

Yield: 6 dozen.

Raspberry-Filled Cookies

These sweet sandwiches use only five ingredients. The raspberry filling peeks from a cutout shape of your choosing.

1 cup butter, softened
½ cup sifted confectioners' sugar
2½ cups all-purpose flour
1 teaspoon vanilla extract
½ cup raspberry preserves

1. Beat the butter at medium speed of an electric mixer until creamy; gradually add the confectioners' sugar, beating until lightly fluffy. Add the flour and vanilla extract, mixing well. Shape the dough into a ball.
2. Roll the dough to ⅛" thickness on a lightly floured surface. Cut with a 2" round cutter. Use a ¾" cutter to cut out a flower or some other decorative design in the center of half of

the cookies. Pierce the solid cookies with the tines of a fork.
3. Place the cookies on ungreased cookie sheets. Bake at 300° for 20 minutes or until the cookies are lightly browned. Cool on wire racks.
4. Spread the top of each solid cookie with about ½ teaspoon raspberry preserves just before serving. Top each with a cutout cookie.

Yield: 3 dozen.

Impeccable Cookies

For great-tasting cookies, preheat the oven 10 minutes before baking, unless otherwise specified. Use shiny baking sheets; dark sheets absorb heat and will cause them to burn. Let cookies cool before storing them. To keep cookies fresh, store chewy cookies in an airtight container and crisp cookies in a jar with a loose-fitting lid.

Served in an elegant sterling-and-crystal sherbet cup, red raspberries and a fresh mint sprig make a refreshing dessert.

Raspberries

With more than 200 species around the world, raspberries are loved because of their intense flavor and aroma. This thorny member of the rose family was deemed an extreme luxury in the mid-nineteenth century when presidential candidate Martin Van Buren was criticized for "wallowing in raspberries." Today, you will find raspberries in recipes for vinegars, sauces, salads, and desserts. However, the best way to eat fresh raspberries is with cream and a splash of sugar.

To preserve this fragile summer fruit for Christmas enjoyment, freeze the berries in a single layer on a jellyroll pan. Pour the frozen raspberries into a heavy-duty plastic bag and store them in the freezer.

Christmas Trifle

This old-fashioned dessert takes a contemporary shortcut when you dress up a bakery pound cake with whipped cream and perfect berries.

CUSTARD SAUCE:
¾ cup sugar
3½ tablespoons cornstarch
A pinch of salt
3 cups milk
3 egg yolks, beaten lightly
2 tablespoons unsalted butter
1 teaspoon vanilla extract

RASPBERRY PUREE:
1 (12-ounce) package frozen dry-pack raspberries, thawed

WHIPPED CREAM:
2½ cups whipping cream
3 tablespoons confectioners' sugar

TRIFLE:
1 (11-ounce) loaf pound cake, cut in ½" slices
¼ cup Grand Marnier, divided
2 pints (about 5 cups) fresh blueberries
2 half-pints (about 3 cups) fresh raspberries
Garnish: fresh raspberries and mint sprigs

TO MAKE CUSTARD SAUCE:
1. In a large saucepan, whisk together the sugar, cornstarch, and salt until blended. Gradually whisk in the milk. Cook over medium-high heat, whisking constantly, until the mixture thickens and boils. Cook and whisk 2 minutes longer. Remove from heat.
2. Reduce heat to medium low. Whisk several large spoonfuls of hot pudding into the egg yolks. Whisk back into the remaining pudding in the saucepan. Cook, whisking constantly, 2 minutes. Remove from heat.
3. Stir in the butter until melted. Stir in the vanilla extract. Pour into a bowl. Press plastic wrap directly on the surface of the sauce.
4. Cool to room temperature, about 3 hours.

TO MAKE RASPBERRY PUREE:
In a food processor, blend the thawed raspberries in several batches, pulsing on/off several times until the berries are liquified. Press through a sieve, discarding the seeds.

TO MAKE WHIPPED CREAM:
In a large mixer bowl, beat the cream at medium-high speed of an electric mixer until cream just begins to hold its shape. Gradually add the confectioners' sugar, beating to stiff peaks.

TO ASSEMBLE:
1. Arrange 1 layer of pound cake slices flat in the bottom of a 4-quart glass bowl, cutting the cake as necessary to fit. Drizzle with 2 tablespoons Grand Marnier and half the raspberry puree.
2. Spread with half the custard sauce. Top with 5 cups blueberries. Spread with 2 cups whipped cream.
3. Top with another layer of pound cake slices. Drizzle with the remaining Grand Marnier and raspberry puree. Spread with the remaining custard sauce. Top with 3 cups fresh raspberries. Spread with 1 cup whipped cream.
4. Using a pastry tube, pipe the remaining whipped cream decoratively around the edge of the trifle. Garnish with the raspberries and mint.
Yield: 12 servings.

Pear and Chocolate Charlotte

Chocolate ladyfingers line the mold of this prime dessert, and glazed pears ring the crown.

CHOCOLATE LADYFINGERS:
⅓   cup all-purpose flour
⅓   cup dark unsweetened cocoa
3   large egg yolks
¼   cup sugar
A few drops of vanilla extract
3   egg whites
¼   cup sugar
Garnish: sifted confectioners' sugar

CHOCOLATE FILLING:
4   large eggs
1   large egg yolk
½   cup water
1   cup sugar
1   pound bittersweet chocolate,
       melted and cooled
3 to 4 tablespoons pear brandy
1¼ cups whipped cream

POACHED PEARS:
2 to 6 (8-ounce) ripe pears, peeled
Sweet wine, such as Sauternes
½   vanilla bean
Juice of 2 lemons, divided

FRUIT GLAZES:
¼   cup apricot jam
2   teaspoons apricot brandy
1¼ cups red currant jelly
2   teaspoons crème de cassis
Garnish: whipped cream, candied
       violets or fresh flowers

TO MAKE CHOCOLATE LADYFINGERS:
1. Butter and flour a baking sheet.
2. Sift together the flour and cocoa. Mix until blended and set aside.
3. In a medium bowl, beat 3 egg yolks and ¼ cup sugar at high speed of an electric mixer until pale yellow, about 5 minutes. Beat in the vanilla extract. Fold in the flour mixture.
4. In a small mixer bowl, beat the egg whites at high speed of an electric mixer until soft peaks form. Gradually add ¼ cup sugar, beating until stiff and glossy.
5. Blend ⅓ of the beaten egg whites into the yolk mixture. Gently fold in the remaining egg whites.
6. Spoon the mixture into a pastry bag with a round ¾" nozzle. Pipe out 22 fingers, 1" wide, 3" long, and ½" thick, in 2 lengthwise rows on a baking sheet. Pipe the fingers side by side so they almost touch.
7. Sprinkle the tops with enough sifted confectioners' sugar to lightly cover. Let stand 2 minutes until the sugar is absorbed. Dust lightly a second time.
8. Sprinkle water on the bottom of the oven. Bake the ladyfingers at 400° for 8 to 10 minutes until a light crust forms.
9. Cool the pan on a wire rack.

TO MAKE CHARLOTTE MOLD:
1. Use a 2-quart Charlotte mold, 7" in diameter, 3½" deep. Line the bottom with a circle of waxed paper, and the sides with waxed paper strips.
2. Line the bottom with 3 Ladyfingers, and the sides with 16 Ladyfingers. (Reserve 3 for the top.)

TO MAKE CHOCOLATE FILLING:
1. In the top of a double boiler, whisk together the eggs, egg yolk, water, and 1 cup sugar. Cook over simmering water, stirring constantly, until the mixture thickens.
2. Remove from the simmering water. Gradually stir in the chocolate. Cool to room temperature, 2 hours.
3. Stir in the pear brandy. Fold in 1¼ cups whipped cream.
4. Pour into the mold. Top with 3 ladyfingers.
5. Cover and refrigerate until firm, 8 hours.

TO MAKE POACHED PEARS:
1. Arrange the pears in a saucepan large enough for the pears to fit on their sides. Add enough wine to cover the pears. Add the vanilla bean and the juice of 1 lemon.
2. Reduce heat, cover, and simmer for 12 to 20 minutes until tender. Turn pears over in the wine mixture.
3. Remove with a slotted spoon. Drizzle with the remaining lemon juice. Drain well.

TO MAKE FRUIT GLAZES:
1. In a saucepan, combine the jam and brandy. Melt over medium heat, stirring often. Sieve and set aside.
2. In another saucepan, combine the jelly and crème de cassis. Melt over medium heat, stirring often. Set aside.

TO ASSEMBLE:
1. Invert the Charlotte Mold onto a serving platter. Remove the waxed paper.
2. Core and halve the Poached Pears. Arrange the pear halves with the stem end toward the center on top of the Charlotte Mold. Brush the pears alternately with apricot and currant glazes.
3. Garnish with whipped cream and candied violets or fresh flowers. Serve in wedges.

   Yield: 12 servings.

Luxurious ribbon wraps this **Pear and Chocolate Charlotte**.

Translated from the French, blancmange means "white food." **White Chocolate Blancmange with Maple-Poached Figs** *is a particularly rich interpretation.*

White Chocolate Blancmange with Maple-Poached Figs

This luscious pudding is molded in custard cups, unmolded into a pool of maple sauce, and topped with white and dark chocolate curls.

WHITE CHOCOLATE BLANCMANGE:

1	envelope unflavored gelatin
¼	cup cold water
1	cup milk
1	vanilla bean, split lengthwise
3	ounces white chocolate, chopped
4	egg yolks
¼	cup sugar
1	cup whipping cream, lightly whipped
2	ounces chopped marrons glacés or candied fruit

MAPLE-POACHED FIGS:

1¼	cups dry red wine
¾	cup maple syrup
8	(1½ to 2 ounce) fresh figs

Garnish: white and dark chocolate curls

TO MAKE WHITE CHOCOLATE BLANCMANGE:

1. Lightly butter 4 (1-cup) custard cups or ramekins.
2. In a small bowl, sprinkle the gelatin over the cold water to soften. Set aside.
3. In a small saucepan, bring the milk and vanilla bean to a boil. Remove from heat. Add the 3 ounces of white chocolate, stirring until melted. Set aside.
4. In a small mixer bowl, beat the egg yolks and sugar at high speed of an electric mixer until thick and lemon colored, about 5 minutes. Gradually strain in the milk mixture, beating at low speed until blended.
5. Pour into a clean small saucepan. Cook over medium-low heat, stirring constantly, until the mixture thickens and coats a spoon. Do not boil. Stir in the softened gelatin until dissolved.
6. Strain into a medium bowl. Press plastic wrap directly on the surface of the custard. Cool to room temperature, about 2 hours.
7. Remove the plastic wrap. Fold in the whipped cream. Refrigerate until partially set, about 10 minutes. Fold in the marrons glacés. Spoon into the custard cups.
8. Cover and refrigerate until set, about 4 hours.

TO MAKE MAPLE-POACHED FIGS:

1. In a deep large saucepan, combine the wine and maple syrup. Bring to a boil. Add the figs. Reduce heat. Cover and simmer until tender, about 5 minutes.
2. Remove the figs with a slotted spoon. Boil the syrup until reduced by half. Pour the syrup into a bowl. Cool until warm, about 45 minutes.
3. To serve, spoon the warm maple-syrup sauce onto 4 large serving plates. Unmold the blancmange onto the sauce. Garnish with chocolate curls.

Yield: 4 servings.

Christmas Spirits

As friends gather to toast the season, offer a festive selection of traditional beverages. For starters, consider:

* *frothy eggnog spiked with rum, whiskey, or brandy*
* *a choice of red or white wine*
* *a full bar complete with beautifully arranged citrus wedges and twists.*

With desserts, serve:

* *fruit liqueur in crystal cordial glasses*
* *champagne in graceful flutes tied with ribbons. Pair a sugary dessert with a dry "brut" champagne, and a tart dessert with a sweeter "sec" or "demi-sec" champagne.*

Layers of semisweet chocolate and white chocolate sandwich the cashew center of **Double Chocolate-Cashew Tart**.

Many a one has been comforted. . .by seeing

a good dish come upon the table.

—*E.C. Gaskell*

Double Chocolate-Cashew Tart

To create heart designs, drop small circles of chocolate around the tart. Then pull the tip of a wooden pick through the circles.

½   (15-ounce) package refrigerated piecrusts
¾   cup semisweet chocolate morsels, melted
1   cup firmly packed brown sugar
½   cup butter or margarine
¼   cup honey
5   tablespoons whipping cream, divided
1   tablespoon vanilla extract
2   large eggs
2   cups chopped lightly salted cashews
3   (2-ounce) white chocolate-flavored baking bars
Semisweet chocolate morsels, melted

1. Roll the piecrust into a 12" circle. Place in an 11" tart pan with removable bottom. Trim off the excess dough around the edges. Spread the melted chocolate over the bottom of the pastry and chill.

2. In a saucepan, combine the sugar, butter, and honey, stir well. Cook over medium-high heat until the butter melts and the sugar dissolves. Bring to a boil; reduce heat, and simmer 2 minutes, stirring occasionally.

3. Remove from heat; stir in 3 tablespoons whipping cream and vanilla extract. Cool 15 minutes.

4. Add the eggs, 1 at a time, beating with a wire whisk after each addition. Stir in the cashews. Pour the mixture into the pastry. Bake at 350° for 20 minutes. Let cool completely on a wire rack.

5. In the top of a double boiler, combine the white chocolate bars and

2 tablespoons whipping cream; bring the water to a boil. Reduce heat to low; cook until the chocolate melts, stirring frequently. Pour the mixture over the tart, spreading to the edges of the pastry.

6. Drop the melted semisweet chocolate in small circles over the white chocolate in the center and around the edge of the tart. Pull the tip of a wooden pick or knife through each circle, forming hearts.

7. Chill 10 minutes or until the chocolate mixture is set. To serve, remove the sides of the tart pan.

Yield: one 11" tart.

A fan of thinly sliced pears brushed with brown sugar covers the silken almond filling of **Caramelized-Pear and Almond Tart**.

Caramelized-Pear and Almond Tart

A too-ripe pear will not slice nicely enough for this elegant tart. Choose unblemished, fragrant fruit with skin that yields to the touch.

DOUGH:
1½ cups all-purpose flour
8   tablespoons cold unsalted butter, cut into bits
2   tablespoons sugar
A pinch of salt
6   tablespoons whipping cream
Dried beans (to weight pastry)

PEAR MIXTURE:
8   ounces almond paste
1   stick unsalted butter, cut into bits
4   teaspoons sugar
2   large eggs
2   tablespoons cake flour, sifted
3   Anjou pears
Melted clarified butter to taste
Granulated brown sugar to taste

TO MAKE DOUGH:
1. In the bowl of an electric mixer fitted with the paddle attachment, combine the flour, butter, sugar, and salt. Blend on low speed until the mixture resembles coarse meal. Add the cream and blend until a dough forms. Chill, covered, 1 hour.

2. Roll out the dough on a lightly floured surface into a circle ⅛" thick. Place in an 11" tart pan with removable bottom and chill 30 minutes.

3. Prick the dough, line it with waxed paper, and weight it with the beans. Bake at 400° for 15 minutes or until the edges are golden. Remove the beans and paper and let the pastry cool to room temperature.

TO MAKE PEAR MIXTURE:
1. In the bowl of an electric mixer fitted with the paddle attachment, beat the almond paste with the butter and sugar until light and fluffy, scraping down the sides of the bowl. Slowly add the eggs, 1 at a time; then beat in the cake flour.

2. Peel and core the pears and cut into thin slices.

TO ASSEMBLE:
1. Transfer the almond mixture to the pastry shell, spreading it into an even layer. Arrange the pear slices on top. Brush the surface of the tart with some of the clarified butter and sprinkle with some of the brown sugar.

2. Bake at 350° for 10 minutes. Brush again with the butter and sprinkle with the sugar. Continue to bake the tart for 45 to 55 minutes or until the almond mixture is firm in the center. If the tart browns too quickly, loosely cover it with foil buttered on one side. Place the buttered side of the foil down over the tart.

3. Transfer the pan to a wire rack. When cool, remove the tart from the pan. Serve the tart with vanilla ice cream, if desired.

Yield: one 11" tart.

Pear Pudding with Caramel Sauce

For a lovely serving, spoon the pudding into crystal goblets. Coat with warm caramel and garnish with chopped pecans.

PUDDING:

⅓ cup butter or margarine, softened
1 cup sugar, divided
2 large eggs
1¼ cups plus ⅓ cup all-purpose flour, divided
1 teaspoon ground cinnamon, divided
¼ teaspoon ground allspice
¼ teaspoon ground nutmeg
½ teaspoon baking soda
½ cup buttermilk
⅓ cup pear preserves
¼ cup butter or margarine, softened

CARAMEL SAUCE:

½ cup sugar
¼ cup butter
½ cup whipping cream
¾ cup chopped pecans, toasted (optional)

TO MAKE PUDDING:

1. Beat ⅓ cup softened butter at medium speed of an electric mixer until creamy; gradually add ½ cup sugar, beating well. Add the eggs, 1 at a time, beating well after each addition. Combine 1¼ cups flour, ½ teaspoon cinnamon, allspice, and nutmeg; stir well. Dissolve the baking soda in the buttermilk. Add the flour mixture to the creamed mixture alternately with the buttermilk mixture, beginning and ending with the flour mixture. Stir in the pear preserves.

2. Pour the batter into a greased and floured 9" square pan. Combine ½ cup sugar, ⅓ cup flour, and ½ teaspoon cinnamon; cut in ¼ cup butter with a pastry blender until the mixture is crumbly.

3. Sprinkle the mixture over the batter. Bake at 350° for 25 minutes or until a wooden pick inserted in the center comes out clean. Cool completely in the pan.

TO MAKE CARAMEL SAUCE:

1. Sprinkle ½ cup sugar into a small cast-iron skillet. Cook over medium heat, stirring constantly with a wooden spoon, until the sugar melts and turns lightly brown. Remove from heat; add ¼ cup butter and stir until blended.

2. Return the mixture to low heat; gradually add the whipping cream to the hot mixture, 2 tablespoons at a time, stirring constantly. Continue to cook the mixture over low heat, stirring constantly, 10 minutes or until mixture is thick and creamy. If desired, stir in the pecans.

3. To serve, cut the pudding into squares and drizzle with the warm Caramel Sauce.

Yield: 9 servings.

Cinnamon Custard Pie

Garnish this pie by sprinkling ground cinnamon over the top and placing a few cinnamon sticks in the center.

2 cups cottage cheese
¼ cup milk
1 cup sugar
3 large eggs, beaten lightly
1 tablespoon all-purpose flour
1 teaspoon vanilla extract
⅛ teaspoon salt
1 unbaked 9" pastry shell
1 teaspoon sugar
½ teaspoon ground cinnamon

1. Combine the cottage cheese and milk in the container of an electric blender; cover and process until smooth, stopping once to scrape down the sides.

2. In a medium bowl, combine the cheese mixture, 1 cup sugar, and next 4 ingredients; stir well. Pour into the pastry shell.

3. Combine 1 teaspoon sugar and cinnamon; stir well. Sprinkle over the cheese mixture. Bake at 450° for 5 minutes. Reduce oven temperature to 350° and bake 25 minutes or until a knife inserted in the center comes out clean. Serve warm or at room temperature.

Yield: one 9" pie.

Now join your hands, and with your hands your hearts.

—Shakespeare

Sweet Potato Pie with Gingersnap Streusel

Sweet potatoes become even sweeter in a gingersnap piecrust.

2   cups gingersnap crumbs
⅓   cup butter or margarine, melted
1   (29-ounce) can sweet potatoes, drained and mashed
1¼   cups evaporated milk
¾   cup firmly packed brown sugar
3   large eggs, beaten lightly
1¼   teaspoons ground cinnamon
1   teaspoon ground allspice
⅔   cup coarsely crushed gingersnaps
⅓   cup firmly packed brown sugar
3   tablespoons all-purpose flour
2   tablespoons butter or margarine, cut into bits
Garnish: sweetened whipped cream

1. Combine 2 cups gingersnap crumbs and ⅓ cup melted butter; stir well. Firmly press the crumb mixture into the bottom and up the sides of a 9½" deep-dish pieplate. Bake at 350° for 6 to 8 minutes. Let cool.
2. Combine the sweet potatoes and the next 5 ingredients; stir well with a wire whisk. Pour the mixture into the crust. Bake at 350° for 20 minutes.
3. Combine ⅔ cup crushed gingersnaps, ⅓ cup brown sugar, and flour; cut in 2 tablespoons butter with a pastry blender until the mixture is crumbly. Sprinkle the streusel over the pie and bake an additional 15 minutes. Cover the pie with foil and bake an additional 25 minutes or until set. Let cool on a wire rack. Garnish with the whipped cream, if desired.
    Yield: one 9½" deep-dish pie.

Prettiest Pies

A gentle touch with pastry brings tender rewards: Handle the dough as little as possible. Roll it out on a floured surface, and dust your hands and the rolling pin with flour. Roll from the center to the edge, working for a thickness of about ⅛".

• Use a soft brush to remove excess flour from the pastry before transferring it to the pieplate.

• Achieve a hand-crimped edge by leaving ½" of the pastry between the rim of the pie and pinching it between your fingers. For a decorative edge on a fruit pie, cut out tiny leaves from pastry scraps and affix them to the rim of the pie with a drop of water, milk, or beaten egg.

• For a shiny, golden finish, brush the crust with milk, beaten egg, or egg whites before baking. To prevent the edge from becoming too brown, cover with a piecrust shield or strips of aluminum foil.

• Cut precise wedges by allowing the pie to cool completely and slicing with a sharp, thin-bladed knife. To keep the point intact, serve with a wedge-shaped pie server.

Chocolate-Raspberry Roulade

A smooth white chocolate layer is rolled into a cake of rich cocoa for a fanciful dessert.

ROULADE:
- ½ cup cocoa
- ¼ cup all-purpose flour
- 4 large eggs, separated
- ¼ teaspoon salt
- 9 tablespoons sugar, divided
- 6 tablespoons seedless raspberry jam, melted and divided
- 2 tablespoons cocoa
- ¾ cup whipping cream, divided
- 4 ounces premium-quality white chocolate, chopped

Garnish: fresh mint sprigs (optional)

RASPBERRY SAUCE:
- 2 (10-ounce) packages frozen raspberries in light syrup, thawed
- 3 tablespoons cornstarch
- 2 teaspoons sugar
- 3 tablespoons Chambord or other raspberry-flavored liqueur
- 2 tablespoons lemon juice

TO MAKE ROULADE:

1. Grease a 15" x 10" x 1" jellyroll pan. Line with waxed paper; grease and flour the waxed paper and the sides of the pan. Set aside.

2. Sift together ½ cup cocoa and flour; set aside.

3. Beat the egg whites and salt at high speed of an electric mixer until foamy; gradually add 6 tablespoons sugar, 1 tablespoon at a time, beating until stiff peaks form and the sugar dissolves (2 to 4 minutes). Set aside.

4. In a large bowl, combine the egg yolks, 3 tablespoons sugar, and 2 tablespoons melted jam; stir well with a wire whisk. Fold in the beaten egg whites. Gently fold in the cocoa mixture until blended. Spread the mixture evenly in the prepared pan. Bake at 350° for 15 minutes.

5. Sift 2 tablespoons cocoa in a 15" x 10" rectangle on a cloth towel. When the cake is done, immediately loosen from the sides of the pan and turn out onto the prepared towel. Peel off the waxed paper. Starting at the narrow end, roll up the cake and towel together; let cool completely on a wire rack, seam side down.

6. In a small saucepan, combine ¼ cup whipping cream and white chocolate; cook over low heat, stirring constantly, until the chocolate melts. Cool completely.

7. In a large bowl, beat remaining ½ cup whipping cream at high speed of an electric mixer until frothy. Gradually add the cooled white chocolate mixture to the whipping cream; beat until thick and smooth. (Mixture may appear curdled, but will smooth as beating continues.)

8. Unroll the cake and remove the towel. Brush the remaining 4 tablespoons melted jam over the cake; spread the white chocolate mixture over the jam. Carefully reroll the cake without the towel; place, seam side down, on a serving plate. Cover and chill at least 1 hour before serving.

9. To serve, spoon 2 tablespoons Raspberry Sauce onto each dessert plate. Cut the roulade into 1" slices; place 1 slice on each plate. Garnish with mint sprigs, if desired. Serve immediately with the remaining Raspberry Sauce.

Yield: 8 servings.

TO MAKE RASPBERRY SAUCE:

1. Place the raspberries in the container of an electric blender or food processor; cover and process until smooth. Pour the mixture through a wire-mesh strainer into a small heavy saucepan; discard the seeds. Add the cornstarch and sugar to the strained mixture, stirring until smooth.

2. Cook over low heat, stirring constantly, until the mixture is thickened. Remove from heat, and stir in the liqueur and lemon juice. Cover and chill thoroughly. Stir before serving.

Yield: 2 cups.

Amaretto-Cream Cheese Pound Cake

An almond-flavored version of a holiday pleasure, this recipe uses amaretto in the place of vanilla.

- 1½ cups butter, softened
- 1 (8-ounce) package cream cheese, softened
- 3 cups sugar
- 7 large eggs
- 3 cups all-purpose flour
- ¼ teaspoon salt
- ½ cup amaretto or other almond-flavored liqueur

Sifted confectioners' sugar (optional)

1. In a large mixing bowl, beat the butter and cream cheese at medium speed of an electric mixer about 2 minutes or until soft and creamy. Gradually add the sugar, beating 2 minutes. Add the eggs, 1 at a time, beating just until yellow disappears after each addition.

2. Combine the flour and salt. Gradually add the flour mixture to the butter mixture alternately with ½ cup amaretto, beginning and ending with the flour mixture. Mix at low speed until blended after each addition.

3. Pour the batter into a greased and floured 12-cup Bundt pan or 10" tube pan. Gently swirl a knife through the batter to remove air pockets.

4. Bake at 325° for 1 hour and 50 minutes or until a wooden pick inserted in the center comes out clean. Cool in the pan on a wire rack 10 to 15 minutes; remove from the pan and let cool completely on a wire rack. Sprinkle with sifted confectioners' sugar, if desired.

Yield: one 10" cake.

Italian Cream Cake

Swirls of rich cream cheese sprinkled with pecans frost this grand three-layer cake.

ITALIAN CREAM CAKE:
1 cup butter or margarine, softened
2 cups sugar
5 large eggs, separated
2½ cups all-purpose flour
1 teaspoon baking soda
1 cup buttermilk
⅔ cup finely chopped pecans
1 teaspoon vanilla extract
1 (3½-ounce) can flaked coconut
½ teaspoon cream of tartar
3 tablespoons light rum

CREAM CHEESE FROSTING:
1 (8-ounce) package cream cheese, softened
1 (3-ounce) package cream cheese, softened
¾ cup butter, softened
1½ (16-ounce) packages confectioners' sugar, sifted
1½ cups chopped pecans
1 tablespoon vanilla extract

TO MAKE ITALIAN CREAM CAKE:
1. Grease and flour 3 (9" round) cakepans. Line the pans with waxed paper; grease the paper and set aside.
2. Beat the butter at medium speed of an electric mixer until creamy; gradually add sugar, beating well. Add the egg yolks, 1 at a time, beating after each addition. Combine the flour and baking soda. Add to the creamed mixture alternately with the buttermilk, beginning and ending with the flour mixture. Stir in the pecans, vanilla extract, and coconut.
3. Beat the egg whites at high speed in a large bowl until foamy. Add the cream of tartar; beat until stiff peaks form. Gently fold the beaten egg whites into the batter. Pour the batter into the prepared pans.
4. Bake at 350° for 25 to 30 minutes or until a wooden pick inserted in the center comes out clean. Let cool in pans 10 minutes. Remove from the pans; peel off the waxed paper and let the cakes cool completely on wire racks. Sprinkle each cake layer with 1 tablespoon light rum. Let stand 10 minutes.
5. To serve, spread the Cream Cheese Frosting between the layers and on the sides and the top of the cake.

TO MAKE CREAM CHEESE FROSTING:
Beat the first 3 ingredients at medium speed of an electric mixer until smooth. Gradually add the confectioners' sugar, beating until light and fluffy. Stir in the pecans and vanilla extract.

Yield: one 3-layer cake.

Custom Cakes

When cooks have mastered a basic cake recipe, they may employ a subtle sleight-of-hand to expand their repertoire without venturing too far from the tried-and-true.

Although a cake recipe's proportion of dry to moist ingredients is best left unchanged, the flavor itself can suit the cook's preference.

Impart a hint of lemon, orange, almond, or rum by substituting those extracts for vanilla, or by using an equal amount of lemon or orange zest, or thawed orange juice or lemonade concentrate.

A layer of sugary rose petals blankets this sumptuous **Eggnog Cheesecake**.

Eggnog Cheesecake

Celebrate the season with this spirited cheesecake splashed with rum and brandy.

CHEESECAKE:

2   cups wheatmeal biscuit crumbs
⅓   cup butter or margarine, melted
2   tablespoons sugar
½   teaspoon ground nutmeg
3   (8-ounce) packages cream cheese, softened
1   cup sugar
1   tablespoon cornstarch
5   large eggs
¾   cup canned or homemade eggnog
¼   cup dark rum
¼   cup brandy

SUGARED ROSE PETALS:

3   large pesticide-free roses
½   cup frozen egg substitute, thawed and beaten lightly
½   cup superfine sugar

TO MAKE CHEESECAKE:

1. Combine the first 4 ingredients; stir well. Firmly press the crumb mixture into the bottom and 1½" up the sides of a lightly greased 9" springform pan. Bake at 325° for 12 to 15 minutes. Remove to a wire rack; let cool.
2. In a large mixer bowl, beat the cream cheese at medium speed of an electric mixer until creamy; gradually add 1 cup sugar and cornstarch, beating well. Add the eggs, 1 at a time, beating after each addition. Stir in the eggnog, rum, and brandy. Pour the batter into the prepared crust.
3. Bake at 325° for 1 hour. (Center will be soft.) Remove from the oven and gently run a knife around the edge of the pan to release the cheesecake from the sides; return to the oven. Turn the oven off; leave the cheesecake in the oven, with the oven door partially opened, 30 minutes. Let cool to room temperature in the pan on a wire rack. Cover and chill 8 hours.
4. To serve, remove the sides of the pan and top the cheesecake with the Sugared Rose Petals, if desired.

Yield: one 9" cheesecake.

TO MAKE SUGARED ROSE PETALS:

1. Pull the petals free from 1 rose. Lightly coat each petal on both sides with the egg substitute, using a small paintbrush.
2. Sift a small amount of the sugar over the coated petals, turning them carefully to coat both sides. Set on waxed paper to dry at least 1 hour. Repeat the procedure with the remaining roses, egg substitute, and sugar.

Yield: 1½ cups.

Petal Crown

To create a small masterpiece, garnish a cake with colorful flowers. From the market, select flowers that are labeled edible, or use edible flowers from your own garden. Be sure they are pesticide-free. Choose nasturtiums, snapdragons, rose petals, pansies, violets, or daylilies.

Frozen White Chocolate Mousse Cake

*This snowy white dessert
rises above a thick
almond-flavored crust.*

CRUST:
½ cup unsalted butter, softened
½ cup sifted confectioners' sugar
½ teaspoon almond extract
¼ cup finely ground blanched
     almonds
1   cup less 2 tablespoons all-purpose
     flour
1   tablespoon cornstarch

CAKE:
2   cups whipping cream, divided
9   ounces good-quality white
     chocolate, chopped
2   tablespoons Crème de Cacao
     liqueur
1   teaspoon almond extract
½ cup sugar
¼ cup water
4   large egg whites

RASPBERRY SAUCE:
1   (10-ounce) package frozen
     raspberries in syrup, thawed
2   tablespoons raspberry jam
2   tablespoons raspberry liqueur

KIWIFRUIT SAUCE:
6   kiwifruit, peeled and quartered
4   tablespoons light corn syrup
2   tablespoons melon liqueur
1   teaspoon unflavored gelatin
Garnish: kiwifruit slices, fresh
     raspberries, and mint leaves

TO MAKE CRUST:
1. In a mixer bowl, beat the butter
and confectioners' sugar with an

electric mixer. Gradually beat in the
almond extract, almonds, flour, and
cornstarch until a soft but not sticky
dough is formed.
2. Press the dough into the bottom of a
9½" springform pan. Chill 30 minutes.
3. Bake at 325° for 30 minutes.
Let cool.

TO MAKE CAKE:
1. In a saucepan set over moderate
heat bring ½ cup of the cream to just
simmering. Reduce the heat to low
and gradually add the chocolate, in
batches, stirring until just melted and
smooth. Transfer the mixture to a
large bowl and stir in the liqueur and
almond extract. Let cool, covered with
plastic wrap, to room temperature.
2. In a small heavy saucepan, combine the sugar and water; bring the
liquid to a boil over medium heat and
stir; simmer until the sugar is dissolved. Boil the syrup, undisturbed,
brushing down the sides of the pan

with cold water, until a candy thermometer registers 238°.
3. In a bowl, beat the egg whites with
an electric mixer until they form soft
peaks. Add the sugar syrup in a stream,
beating until cool, about 5 minutes.
4. Stir ¼ of the meringue into the
chocolate mixture and fold in
the remaining meringue gently but
thoroughly.
5. In a bowl, beat the remaining
cream with an electric mixer until
soft peaks form. Fold the cream into
the chocolate mixture.
6. Transfer the mousse to the prepared
crust and freeze it, covered with plastic wrap, for 5 hours or until set. The
mixture will keep for up to 1 week.
7. To serve, coat half a dessert plate
with Raspberry Sauce and half with
Kiwifruit Sauce. Center a slice of
mousse cake on top. Garnish with the
kiwifruit slices, raspberries, and mint.
   Yield: 12 servings.

TO MAKE RASPBERRY SAUCE:
In a food processor, puree the raspberries and jam. Press the puree
through a fine sieve into a bowl. Stir
in the liqueur. Cover and chill.
   Yield: 1 cup.

TO MAKE KIWIFRUIT SAUCE:
1. In a food processor, puree the
kiwifruit. Press the puree through a fine
sieve into a bowl. Add the corn syrup
and melon liqueur and stir to combine.
2. Transfer to a small saucepan and
stir in the gelatin. Let stand five minutes. Cook over low heat, stirring,
until the gelatin dissolves. Transfer to
a bowl. Cover and chill.
   Yield: 1 cup.

Garnished with flowers to match the table setting (opposite), **Frozen White Chocolate Mousse Cake** *is superb with a cup of steaming coffee.*

BEESWAX CANDLE-MAKING SUPPLIES:
Pourette Manufacturing Company
1418 NW 53rd Street, P.O. Box 17056
Seattle, WA 98107
(800) 888-9425

DECORATIVE RUBBER STAMPS:
Personal Stamp Exchange
360 Sutton Place
Santa Rosa, CA 95407
For stores in your area, call
(707) 588-8058.

DRESSMAKER'S BUILLION (CRINKLE WIRE) & TRIMS:
D. Blumchen & Company
162 East Ridgewood Avenue,
P.O. Box 1210-VC
Ridgewood, NJ 07451-1210
(201) 652-5595

ESSENTIAL OILS:
The Essential Oil Company
P.O. Box 206
Lake Oswego, OR 97034
(800) 729-5912

EVERGREEN TREES, GARLANDS, AND WREATHS:
Laurel Springs Christmas Tree Farm
Highway 18 South, P.O. Box 85
Laurel Springs, NC 28644-0085
(800) 851-2345

FABRIC:
Waverly
79 Madison Avenue
New York, NY 10016
For stores in your area, call
(800) 423-5881.

FLOWER BULBS:
White Flower Farms
P.O. Box 50
Litchfield, CT 06759-9952
(800) 503-9624

HANDMADE PAPERS:
Loose Ends
3824 River Road
Keizer, OR 97307
(800) 390-9979

HERBS AND DRIED NATURALS:
Tom Thumb Workshops
14100 Lankford Hwy. Rt. 13,
P.O. Box 357
Mappsville, VA 23407
(757) 824-3507

HYACINTH VASES:
Gardener's Eden
P.O. Box 7307
San Francisco, CA 94120-7307
(800) 822-9600

PAPERS AND STICKERS FOR DECOUPAGE:
The Gifted Line
999 Canal Boulevard
Point Richmond, CA 94804
For stores in your area, call
(800) 5-GIFTED.

RIBBON:
Midori, Inc.
3524 West Government Way
Seattle, WA 98199
For stores in your area, call
(206) 282-3595.

C.M. Offray & Son, Inc.
360 Route 24
Chester, NJ 07930
(908) 879-4700

SEALING WAX AND BRASS STAMPS:
Victorian Papers
P.O. Box 411341
Kansas City, MO 64141
(800) 800-6647

STYROFOAM SPHERES AND BRICKS:
Schrock's International
110 Water Street, P.O. Box 538
Bolivar, OH 44612
(330) 874-3700

WHOLE AND GROUND SPICES:
Spice, Etc.
P.O. Box 5266
Charlottesville, VA 22905
(800) 827-6373

Madelyn Andruk for Mecox Gardens
Pages 31, 64

Mary Baltz
Pages 42, 93

Van Bankston
Page 80

Judy Blackman for Zen
Flowers on pages 6, 96

Cedar Grove Plantation Bed & Breakfast
Edgefield, SC
Frozen White Chocolate Mousse Cake, page 138

Flowering Design
Greenery on pages 22, 33, 42, 62, 91, 93

Margaret Furlong
Pages 44–45, 47

Charlotte Hagood
Page 38

The Inn at Blackberry Farm
Walland, TN
Black and Green Olives in Citrus-Mustard Vinaigrette, Cranberry-Walnut Relish, Corn Relish, page 111

Susan Kochman, New England Catering Company
Cornwall Bridge, CT
Mapled Brussels Sprouts, page 108

The Lygon Arms
Worchestershire, England
White Chocolate Blancmange with Maple-Poached Figs, page 129

Mansion on Turtle Creek Hotel and Restaurant
Dallas, TX
Roast Goose with Molasses Glaze and Apricot Stuffing, page 102

Debbie Maugans
Green Beans with Balsamic-Glazed Onions, page 107
Chocolate-Raspberry Roulade, page 134

Michael Mitrano
Pages 60–61

Heather Mull
Page 52

Lelia Gray Neil
Page 27

Old World Christmas
Page 2

Charlie Palmer, Aureole
New York, NY
Caramelized-Pear and Almond Tart, page 131

Carol S. Richard
Pages 40, 63

Richmond Hill Inn
Asheville, NC
Herb-Glazed Turkey with Wild Mushroom and Leek Stuffing, page 105
Corn Pudding with Crabcake Topping, page 106
Sour Cream Pound Cake with Dried Fruit Compote, page 114

The Royal Crescent Hotel
Bath, England
Miniature Mince Pies, page 118
Scones, page 121

Joedda Sampson, Cafe Victoria
Pittsburgh, PA
Potato and Pear Tart, page 108

Scaff Floral Creations
Flowers on page 41

Janice Schindeler
Page 70

Betsy Scott
Pages 50–51

Sugar Hill Wreaths
Greenery on pages 28–29

Sybil Sylvester
Pages 56–57, 59

Elizabeth Taliaferro
Pages 66–69, 72, 74

Carol M. Tipton
Page 54

Emelie Tolley
Thyme Biscuits with Red Currant Jelly, page 112
Orange-Rosemary Pinwheels, page 112

Raymond Waites
Page 23

Ron Wendt
Flowers on page 81

Peggy Ann Williams
Page 48

PHOTOGRAPHERS

Ralph Anderson
Pages 68–70, 72, 74, 99, 101, 107, 130

Jim Bathie
Pages 36, 43 (left), 66, 136

Hedrich Blessing
Pages 114–115

Pierre Chanteau
Pages 55, 83 (top)

Van Chaplin
Pages 34, 63

Rick Dean
Pages 19, 38

Christopher Drake
Page 128

Colleen Duffley
Page 122

Tom Eckerle
Page 49

Joshua Greene
Pages 120, 127

Gross & Daley
Pages 78–80, 138–139

Jim Hedrich
Page 104

Brit Huckabay
Page 77

John Kane
Page 18

Katrina
Page 32

James Merrell
Page 84

Starr Ockenga
Pages 12, 30, 90

John O'Hagan
Pages 10–11, 26–27, 40, 48, 50–51, 54, 56–57, 59

Toshi Otsuki
Cover and pages 2, 5, 9, 16, 21–25, 31, 37, 42, 43 (right), 60–61, 64, 81 (right), 82, 88, 92 (bottom), 93, 98, 109, 116–117, 119, 123, 129, 131, 144

Luciana Pampalone
Page 92 (top)

Steve Randazzo
Pages 41 (left), 52, 85–87

Michael Skott
Pages 44–45, 47

William P. Steele
Pages 6, 15, 17, 28–29, 33, 41 (right), 46, 62, 81 (left), 83 (bottom), 89 (all), 91, 94–96, 102, 110, 113, 124, 133

PHOTO STYLISTS

Julie Azar
Page 34

Mary Baltz
Page 81 (left)

Roscoe Betsill
Page 83

Susan George-Calsmer
Page 30

Kay E. Clarke
Page 136

Virginia R. Cravens
Pages 68–74, 77, 99, 101, 107, 130

Tova Cubert
Pages 19, 38

Michelle Berriedale-Johnson
Page 84

Marjorie Johnston
Pages 43, 66

Katie Stoddard
Pages 10–11, 26-27, 36, 40, 48, 50–51, 54, 56–57, 59, 63

Linda Baltzell Wright
Pages 50–51, 56–57, 59

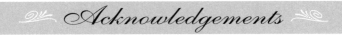

Acknowledgements

Kimberley Bealle
Nicole Esposito
David Graff
Jenifer Kramer
Fran Reilly
Risa Turken